D1750227

Epitaphs: A Unique Collection of Post Mortem Comment, Obituary Wit, Quaint and Gruesome Fancy

Frederic William Unger

Copyright © BiblioLife, LLC

BiblioLife Reproduction Series: Our goal at BiblioLife is to help readers, educators and researchers by bringing back in print hard-to-find original publications at a reasonable price and, at the same time, preserve the legacy of literary history. The following book represents an authentic reproduction of the text as printed by the original publisher and may contain prior copyright references. While we have attempted to accurately maintain the integrity of the original work(s), from time to time there are problems with the original book scan that may result in minor errors in the reproduction, including imperfections such as missing and blurred pages, poor pictures, markings and other reproduction issues beyond our control. Because this work is culturally important, we have made it available as a part of our commitment to protecting, preserving and promoting the world's literature.

All of our books are in the "public domain" and some are derived from Open Source projects dedicated to digitizing historic literature. We believe that when we undertake the difficult task of re-creating them as attractive, readable and affordable books, we further the mutual goal of sharing these works with a larger audience. A portion of BiblioLife profits go back to Open Source projects in the form of a donation to the groups that do this important work around the world. If you would like to make a donation to these worthy Open Source projects, or would just like to get more information about these important initiatives, please visit www.bibliolife.com/opensource.

EPITAPHS

A unique collection of post mortem comment, obituary wit, and quaint and gruesome fancy

By

FREDERIC W. UNGER

Philadelphia
The Penn Publishing Company
1905

Classification

INTRODUCTION	5
UNCONSCIOUS HUMOR	7
DELIBERATE HUMOR	22
CONJUGAL EPITAPHS	43
DEROGATORY	52
EPITAPHS ON OCCUPATIONS	73
CONVERSATIONAL EPITAPHS	83
PUNNING EPITAPHS	88
BACCHANALIAN	93
EPITAPHS ON INFANTS AND CHILDREN . .	95
BRIEF EPITAPHS	101
PATHETIC EPITAPHS	105
EPITAPHS ON CELEBRATED PERSONS . . .	113
MISCELLANEOUS EPITAPHS	129
EPITAPHS BY "MAX ADELER"	165

Introduction

PRESENT day conditions of public feeling, aided by an almost universal censorship conducted by cemetery authorities, has practically ended the manufacture of absurd epitaphs.

In compiling a work of this kind it is therefore obvious that the major part of its contents are, to say the least, not modern. Also that some of the collection has previously appeared in previous publications.

However, a large number of previously unpublished epitaphs have been obtained, to which are added many which have only appeared before in rare publications, long out of print.

Certain epitaphs, by their frequent publication, have become accepted classics in graveyard literature and could not with propriety be excluded from as complete a collection as this.

Of these latter there are many variants, for they have been copied and recopied from cemetery to cemetery in all parts of the world. An

INTRODUCTION

effort has been made to present only the best forms of this class.

Many important epitaphs have never been actually engraved upon tombs, but have appeared as obituary notices in periodicals or in the writings of recognized authors of standing. Still others have appeared in works of fiction, or without pretense of validity have been published in other mediums. Their presence here is chiefly valuable as instancing the validity of the adage—"Truth is stranger than fiction." Their wit or absurdity is often less than that of epitaphs of undisputed authenticity.

Being familiar with the majority of previous publications on this subject, the compiler of this volume does not hesitate to recommend it as the most complete, comprehensive, and careful selection of odd, grotesque and striking epitaphs yet presented to the public.

Acknowledgments are made to Alexander H. Laidlaw, Jr., of New York City, for the use of private collections and other assistance in making this collection.

FREDERIC WM. UNGER.

Philadelphia, July 1, 1904.

Unconscious Humor

To
The Memory of
John Phillips
Accidentally Shot
as
A Mark of Affection by His
Brother.

From St. Nicholas', Yarmouth:
Here lyeth ye body of
SARAH BLOOMFIELD,
Aged 74
Cut off in blooming yuthe we can but

In New Jersey:
Julia Adams
Died of thin shoes, April 17th, 18:
aged 19 years.

In Plymouth churchyard:

>Here lies the body of
>Thomas Vernon,
>The only *surviving* son of
>Admiral Vernon.

New Berne, North Carolina:

Ingenious youth, thou art laid in dust.
Thy friends, for thee, in tears did burst.

From Montmartre cemetery:

>Here lies A. B.
>Who at the age of eighteen
>earned £40 a year.

Over the grave of a musical composer were the lines —

>He has gone to the only place where
>His own works are excelled.

This was copied by the widow of a pyrotechnics manufacturer, as follows:

>Erected by his spouse
to the memory of
A—— B——
Manufacturer of Fireworks.
He has gone to the only place
Where his own works are excelled.

The widow of a man who was blown to pieces by gunpowder, insisted that the following be written above his gathered fragments:

He rests in pieces.

John Palfryman, who is buried here
Was aged four and twenty year,
And near this place his mother lies
Likewise his father when he dies.

Ledyard, Conn., on a man who died of natural causes after several attempts at suicide:

He died an honest death.

On a missionary in India:
Here lies the body of the Rev. T. Henry, M. A.,
who long laboured as a Christian missionary
amongst the Rajputs.
He was shot by his chokedar.
"Well done, good and faithful servant."

A marble-cutter, inscribing the words,—"Lord, she was thine" upon a tombstone, found that he had not figured his spaces correctly and he reached the end of the stone one letter short. The epitaph therefore read:

"Lord, she was thin."

The following is an extract from a letter received at the Pension Office at Washington:

"As I married three soldiers, I don't see how you can git out of holding that I am the widow of at least one of them. I done my duty to one and all of them, and I laid them out side by side, as you can see by visiting the sometry at Oke Hill, where they lay at rest under their names and dates, with one poem covering all.

"O Lord, who maketh man to live
For but a fleating day,
You have it in Your power to give
As well as take away."

A marble-cutter, not having sufficient room upon the stone for the desired epitaph,—"Let her rest in peace!" abbreviated it thus:
"Let her R. I. P."

From Germantown, Pa.:
Here lies the dust of Louisa Orr, whose soul is now a little ANGLE in Heaven.

Here lies Peter Montgomery, who was accidentally shot in his 30th year. This monument was erected by *grateful* relatives.

From Colorada:
Bill Jenkins. Died June 13, 1901.
He done his damn'dest damn'dest. Angels could do no more.

From a churchyard in Rothesay:
Erected by JANE ———,
to the memory of her husband JOHN ———.
"Him that cometh unto me I will in no wise cast out."

From a churchyard in Pembrokeshire:
Here lie I, and no wonder I'm dead,
For the wheel of the waggon went over my head.

On a maid of honor:
    Here lies (the Lord have mercy on her)
    One of Her Majesty's maids of honour:
    She was young, slender, and pretty;
    She died a maid—the more's the pity.

South Dennis, Mass.:
Of seven sons the Lord his father gave,
He was the fourth who found a watery grave.
Fifteen days had passed since the circumstance occurred,
When his body was found and decently interred.

On a tombstone at Florence is this inscription:
    Here lies SALVINO ARMOLO D'ARMATI,
        of Florence,
      the inventor of spectacles.
     May God pardon his sins!
        The year 1318.

EPITAPHS

Colorado:

    He was young
    He was fair
    But the Injuns
    Raised his hair.

Poor Betty Conway
She drank lemonade
At a masquerade
So now she's dead and gone away.

Here lies Dame Dorothy Peg,
Who never had issue except in her leg,
So great was her art, so deep was her cunning,
That while one leg stood, the other kept running

In a Scotch graveyard:

Here—lies my guid and gracious auntie,
Wham death has packed in his portmanty,
Three score years and ten did God gift her,
And here she lies, wha deil daurs lift her?

On a Locomotive:

    Collisions four or five she bore
    The signals were in vain,
    Grown old and rusted,
    Her biler busted—
    And smashed the excursion train.

    Here I lays
    Killed by a chaise.

From Pewsey churchyard in Dorsetshire:

Here lies the body
of
LADY O'LOONEY,
Great niece of Burke,
Commonly called the Sublime.
She was
Bland, passionate, and deeply religious,
Also she painted
In water-colors,
And sent several pictures
To the Exhibition.
She was first cousin
To Lady Jones,
And of Such
Is the Kingdom of Heaven.

Maryland:
>Elizabeth Scott lies buried here.
>She was born Nov. 20th, 1785,
>according to the best of her recollection.

Burlington, Va.:
>Died when young and full of promise
>Of whooping cough our Thomas.

In a Pennsylvania churchyard:
>Eliza, sorrowing, rears this marble slab
>To her dear JOHN, who died of eating crab.

The following is in the Necropolis, Glasgow:
>Here lyes Bessy Bell,
>But whereabouts I cannot tell.

From Montrose churchyard:

Here lies the bodeys of George Young and Isbel Guthrie, and all their posterity for fifty years backwards.   November, 1757.

From Nettlebed churchyard, Oxfordshire:
Here lies father, and mother, and sister, and I:
　We all died within the space of one short year:
They were all buried at Wimble except I,
　And I be buried here.

At Fosbrooke, in Northumberland:
　Here lieth Matthew Hollingshead,
　Who died from cold caught in his head.
　It brought on fever and rheumatiz,
　Which ended me—for here I is.

From a cemetery near Cincinnati:
　　Here lies ———
　Who came to this city and died
　　for the benefit of his health.

From Belturbet churchyard, Ireland:
　　Here lies JOHN HIGLEY,
　whose mother and father were drowned
　　in their passage from America.
Had they both lived they would have been buried
　　　　here.

Broom churchyard, Bedfordshire:
>God be praised

Here is Mr. Dudley senior, and Jane his wife also;
Who while living was his superior, but see what death can do.
Two of his sons also lie here, One Walter, t'other Joe;
They all of them went—in the year
>1510—below.

From St. Philip's churchyard, Birmingham:
× To the memory of James Baker, who died January 27th, 1781.
>O cruel Death, how cou'd you be so unkind
>To take him before and leave me behind?
>You should have taken both of us, if either,
>Which would have been more pleasing to the survivor.

Block Island, N. Y.:
>>He's done a catching cod
>>And gone to meet his God.

Tennessee:

She lived a life of virtue and died of the cholera morbus, caused by eating green fruit in hope of a blessed immortality.

Reader, go thou and do likewise.

Samuel Gardner was blind in one eye and in a moment of confusion he stepped out of a receiving and discharging door in one of the warehouses into the ineffable glories of the celestial sphere.

Wayland:

Here lies the body of Dr. Hayward,
A man who never voted.
Of such is the kingdom of Heaven.

Father and Mother and I
Choose to be buried asunder,
Father and Mother here,
And I buried yonder.

Greenwood, N. Y.:

> Grieve not for me my Harriet dear
>   For I am better off,
> You know what were my sufferings,
>   And what a dreadful cough.

Alexandria, Va.:

(Mr. James Danner, late of Louisville, having been laid by the side of his four wives received this touching epitaph.)

  An excellent husband was this Mr. Danner,
He lived in a thoroughly honorable manner,
    He may have had troubles,
    But they burst like bubbles,
He's at peace now, with Mary, Jane, Susan and Hannah.

Pembroke, New Hampshire:

    Here lies a man
    Never beat by a plan,
    Straight was his aim
    And sure of his game.
    Never was a lover
    And invented a revolver.

The manner of her death was thus
She was druv over by a bus.

On the twenty second of June,
Jonathan Fiddle went out of tune.
					BEN JOHNSON.

The following is taken from a head-board at a grave in the Sparta Diggings, California; and, taking the orthography into consideration, it is an unconscious blending of the serio-comic with the would-be sublime:

In memory ov
JOHN SMITH, who met
wierlent death neer this spot
18 hundred and 40 too. He was shot
by his own pistill;
It was not one of the new kind,
but a old fashioned
brass barrel, and of such is the
Kingdom of heaven.

Here lies the body of MOLLY DICKIE, the Wife of HALL DICKIE, tailor

    Two great physicians first
    My Loving husband tried,
    To cure my pain——
    In vain,
    At last he got a third,
    And then I died.

    Him as was, is gone from we,
      So we as is, must go to he.

In West churchyard, Tranent, England:
    Trumpets shall sound,
    And archangels cry,
    "Come forth, Isabel Mitchell,
    And meet Wm. Matheson in the sky."

St. Giles churchyard, Northampton:
    Here lies a most dutiful daughter,
      Honest and just,
    Awaiting the resurrection in hopes,
      To be one of the first.

Deliberate Humor

Written over the entrance to a cemetery:
Here lie the dead and here the living *lie*.

    Little boy,
        Pair of skates,
    Broken Ice,
        Golden Gates.

    Little girl,
        Box of paints,
    Sucked her brush,
        Joined the Saints.

    Bigger boy,
        Sea gull's nest,
    Rumbling rocks,
        Eternal rest.

    Bigger girl,
        Healthy bloom,
    Belt too tight,
        Early tomb.

Eastwell cemetery, Kent:
>Fear God,
>Keep the commandments,
>and
>Don't attempt to climb a tree,
>For that's what caused the death of me.

At Huntingdon:
>On the 29th of November
>A confounded piece of timber
>Came down, bang slam,
>And killed I, John Lamb.

Here lie several of the Stowes,
Particulars the last day will disclose.

In Cheltenham churchyard:
>ˣ Here lies I and my two daughters,
>Killed by drinking Cheltenham waters;
>If we had stuck to Epsom salts,
>We shouldn't be lying in these here vaults.

From Burlington churchyard, Mass.:

Here lies the body of Mary Ann Lowder;
She burst whilst drinking a seidlitz powder;
Called from this world to her heavenly rest,
She should have waited till it effervesced.

By Dr. Goldsmith, on Mr. Edward Pardon:

Here lies poor NED PARDON, from misery freed,
Who long was a bookseller's hack;
He led such a damnable life in this world,
I don't think he'll ever come back.

She sought for aid and sought in vain,
Physicians could not cure her pain.
Her pains were those that can't be cured,
No office had her life insured.

What is life? 'Tis but a vision!
I met death in a collision.
Twenty more died by the same.
Verdict—Nobody to blame!

Many stood round, but none could save
The blooming youth from a watery grave.
But, after a time, the corpse did rise
And eager friends did seize the prize.

EPITAPHS

Gone to meet his mother-in-law!

On an ossified man:
>   He died hard.

A. D. 1827: I am anxiously expecting you.
A. D. 1867: Here I am.

From Lost Creek, Colorado:
  Here lies the clay of Mitchell Coots,
  Whose feet yet occupy his boots.
  His soul has gone—we know not where
  It landed, neither do we care.
  He slipped the joker up his sleeve
  With vile intention to deceive,
  And when detected, tried to jerk
  His gun, but didn't get his work
  In with sufficient swiftness, which
  Explains the presence here of Mitch.
  At Gabriel's trump, if he should wake,
  He'll mighty likely try to take
  The trump with that same joker he
  Had sleeved so surreptitiously,
  And which we placed upon his bier
  When we concealed his body here.

Thomas Parr, the well-known centenarian, had a son of the same name. The latter, who was past eighty when he died, has this epitaph:
Here lies the body of Thomas Parr.
What, old Tom ? No. Why, young Tom ? Ah !

   ×Listen ! Mother, aunt and me
     Were killed sudden. Here we be.
     We should have no time to missle
     Had they blown the engine's whistle.

An epitaph read:
   *Here I lie snug as a bug in a rug.
An envious relative directed that he be buried in an adjoining grave with the following inscription over him:
   Here I lie snugger than that other bugger.

   ' He got a fish bone in his throat
     And then he sang an angel's note.

Poor Martha Snell ! her's gone away,
   Her would if her could, but her couldn't stay ;
   Her'd two sore legs and a baddish cough,
   But her leg it was as carried her off.

EPITAPHS

Vineyard Haven:

John and Lydia, that blooming pair,
  A whale killed him and her body lies here.

Bayfield, Miss.:

  Stranger pause, my tale attend,
    And learn the cause of Hannah's end.
    Across the world the wind did blow,
    She ketched a cold that laid her low.
    We shed a lot of tears 't is true,
    But life is short—aged 82.

Here lies the body of Mary Ann Bent,
  She kicked up her heels, and away she went.

On Roger Norton, Cornwall:

Here lies, alas! poor Roger Norton,
  Whose sudden death was oddly brought on:
  Trying one day his corns to mow off,
  The razor slipped and cut his toe off!
  The toe, or rather what it grew to,
  An inflammation quickly flew to;
  The part then took to mortifying,
  Which was the cause of Roger's dying.

The winter snow congealed his form
But now we know our Uncle's warm.

Here lies the body of Jonathan Near
Whose mouth it stretched from ear to ear.
Tread softly, stranger, o'er this wonder,
For if he yawns, you're gone, by thunder!

Old Vicar Sutor lieth here
Who had a Mouth from ear to ear,
Reader, tread lightly on the sod,
For if he gapes, you're gone, by G——.

In Ballyporen (Ire.) churchyard, on Teague O'Brian, written by himself:

Here I at length repose
My spirit now at aise is;
With the tips of my toes
And the point of my nose
Turned up to the roots of the daisies.

From New Jersey:

Weep, stranger, for a father spilled
From a stage coach and nearly killed,
His name was John Sykes, a maker of sassengers,
Slain with three other outside passengers.

On old Jeremiah who died in Gray's Inn Lane Work House:

Old Jerry's dead at last (God rest his soul)
His body's shoveled down some work-house hole,
Or else to Doctors given for dissection.
His spirit has gone to Old Nick for correction,
And his old clothes to spread some new infection.

From Llangerrig churchyard, Montgomeryshire:

    From earth my body first arose
    But here to earth again it goes
    I never desire to have it more
    To plague me as it did before.

An honest fellow here is laid
His debts in full he always paid,
And what's more strange, the neighbors tell us
He brought back borrowed umbrellas.

St. Botolph's:

    A traveller lies here at rest
    Who life's rough ocean tossed on.
    His many virtues all expressed
    Thus simply—" *I'm from Boston.*"

From a tombstone in Connecticut:

Here lies cut down like unripe fruit,
The wife of Deacon Amos Shute:
She died of drinking too much coffee,
Anny Dominy eighteen forty.

Here lies the body of Jonathan Stout.
He fell in the water and never got out,
And still is supposed to be floating about.

He never won immortal fame
Nor conquered earthly ills
But men weep for him all the same
He always paid his bills.

Skaneateles, N. Y.:

Neuralgia worked on Mrs. Smith
'Till neath the sod it laid her.
She was a worthy Methodist
And served as a crusader.

On a man who was killed by a pump:

JOHN ADAMS.

Here lies JOHN ADAMS, who received a thump
Right on the forehead from the parish pump,
Which gave him the quietus in the end,
For many doctors did his case attend.

Mock epitaph written on door of Charles II's bedroom:

> Here lies our sovereign lord the king,
>   Whose word no man relies on;
> Who never said a foolish thing,
>   And never did a wise one.
> EARL OF ROCHESTER.

The king on reading the above said, "It is very true; my doings are those of my ministers, but my sayings are my own," thus turning the jest on Rochester.

Childwell, England:

> Here lies the body of
>   JOHN SMITH.
> Buried in the cloisters
> If he don't jump at the last trump,
>   Call, Oysters!

From New Jersey:

> She was not smart, she was not fair,
>   But hearts with grief for her are swellin';
> All empty stands her little chair:
>   She died of eatin' water-melon.

From a churchyard near Salisbury on a man named Button:

Oh! Sun, Moon, Stars, and ye celestial Poles
Are graves then dwindled into button-holes?

From the Baltimore Sun:

    He heard the angels calling him
        From the celestial shore,
    He flapped his wings and away he went
        To make one angel more.

Here lies the body of G<small>EORDIE</small> D<small>ENHAM</small>,
If ye saw him now ye wadna ken him.

Here lies the body of our Jean
None in the parish half so mean
She stayed in bed her clothes to save
And nearly drowned to save a grave,
When we all rise on Judgment Day
She'll lie still if there's aught to pay.

Here lies the body of Moses Worth
Small of head and small of girth,
He lied in life, he lies in death —
He lied himself clean out of breath.

Josephine lies here below,
Upon my word she was not slow,
The life she led was very sporty —
She died when she was nearly forty.

Mason, Elk, and Mystic Shriner —
Georgie was a steady jiner,
He jined what e'er a jiner should,
He jined most everything he could.
He jined the good, he jined the ill,
It's safe to say he's jining still —
Where he has gone, we do not know,
Perhaps he's jining things below.

Skaneateles, New York:

Underneath this pile of stones
Lies all that's left of Sally Jones.
Her name was Lord, it was not Jones,
But Jones was used to rhyme with stones.

And this variant:

Here lies JOHN BUNN,
Who was killed by a gun.
His name wasn't Bunn, but his real name was WOOD,
But Wood wouldn't rhyme with gun, so I thought Bunn should.

Also:

Underneath this ancient pew
Lie the remains of Jonathan BLUE;
His name was BLACK, but that wouldn't do

And this:
Here lie the remains of Thomas Wood*hen*,
The most amiable of husbands and excellent o
    men.
N. B.   His real name was Wood*cock*, but it
Wouldn't come in rhyme.—*His widow.*

Here lies the body of Jonathan Ground
Who was lost at sea and never found.

In a churchyard near Canterbury:
Of children in all she bore twenty-four:
Thank the Lord there will be no more.

Here lies John Ross,
Kick'd by a hoss.

Man's life's a vapor, and full of woes,
He cuts a caper, and down he goes.

˟ A bird, a man, a loaded gun,
No bird, dead man, Thy will be done.

From Cornwall, England:
⁺ Here lies the body of Gabriel John
Who died in the year 1601.
Pray for the soul of Gabriel John,
You may if you please, or let it alone,
  For it's all one
   To Gabriel John,
Who died in the year 1601.

On one too poor to purchase burial space *within* the church:
˟ Here I lie at the Church door,
Here I lie because I'm poor,
When I rise at the Judgment Day,
I shall be as warm as they.
Pencilled underneath was found —
  From a spirit within (the church)
' Tis true old sinner there you lie,
' Tis true you'll be as warm as I,
But restless spirit, why foretell —
That when you rise, you'll go to H——?

In an Eastern Pennsylvania churchyard:
  Little Willie, he was our lily,
  God for him sent, and we let him went.
Underneath in pencil was written —
  One can't always sometimes tell,
  Willie may have went to H——.

From a Suffolk County churchyard, England:
  Here lies the body of Mary Ann,
  Who rests in the bosom of Abraham.
Underneath some wag had pencilled:
  It's all very nice for Mary Ann
  But it's mighty tough on Abraham.

By a man who was probably impressed with the uselessness of the fulsome epitaphs of his locality:
  Here lies the body of Stearnhold Oakes
  Who lived and died like other folks.

In Oxfordshire—A trifle previous:
  Here lies the body of John Eldred,
  At least, he will be here when he's dead;
  But now at this time he is alive,
  The 14th of August, Sixty-five.

On a Mr. Foote, of Norwich:

    Here lies a Foote
    Whose death may thousands save;
    For Death has now one foot
    Within the grave.

On a Mr. Fish:

    Worms are bait for fish
    But here's a sudden change,
    Fish is bait for worms —
    Is not that passing strange?

In St. George's churchyard, Somerset:

    Here lies poor Charlotte,
    Who was no harlot,
    But in her virginity
    Though just turned nineteen —
    Which within this vicinity,
    Is hard to be found and seen.

East Thompson, N. Y.:

Here lies one who never sacrificed his reason to superstitious God, nor ever believed that Jonah swallowed the whale.

Peter letig was his name
Heaven I hope his station,
Baltimore his dwelling place,
And Christ is his salvation.

Grafton, Vt.:
    Gone Home Below

Added by his widow and executrix—
To follow you I'm not content,
Unless I know which way you went.

A zealous locksmith died of late,
And did arrive at heaven's gate;
He stood without and would not knock,
Because he meant to pick the lock.

Here lies Richard Dent
In his last tenement.

Here lies Tommy Day
Removed from over the way.

No doctor ever physicked me,
Was never near my side.
But when fever came I thought of the name,
And that was enough—I died.

Avon, Mass.:

Consumption come, God's will be done,
Let every sinner cease;
To Jesus fly, prepare to die,
And find eternal peace.

Maryland:

My father and mother were both insane
I inherited the terrible stain.
My grandfather, grandmother, aunts and uncles
Were lunatics all, and yet died of carbuncles.

Keesville, N. Y.:

Here lies a man of good repute
Who wore a No. 16 Boot
'Tis not recorded how he died,
But sure it is that open wide
The gates of heaven must have been
To let such monstrous feet within.

Here lies Sir John Plumpudding of the Grange,
Who hanged himself one morning for a change.

Sarah Thomas is dead and that's enough,
The candle is out and so is the snuff
Her soul is in Heaven you need not fear
And all that's left is buried here.

Wyoming County, N. Y.:
She was in health at 11.30 A. M.
And left for Heaven at 3.30 P. M.

Ithaca, N. Y.:
The pale consumption gave the fatal blow.
The fate was certain although the event was slow.

Tread softly mortals o'er the bones
Of this world's wonder, Captain Jones,
Who told his glorious deeds to many
Yet never was believed by any.
Posterity let this suffice
He swore all's true, yet here he lies.

Here lies the body of John Bidwell,
Who, when in life, wished his neighbors no evil.
  In hopes up to jump
  When he hears the last trump
And triumph over Death and the Devil.

  Here lies the body of Dr. Bowen
  Caught when death was out a mowin',
      Used to curing others' ills —
      Yet his homeopathic pills,
  Couldn't keep the Doc from goin'.

Over a tragedian:
    Taking off this awful actor
    Death was here a benefactor.

Here lies the body of our Anna
Done to death by a banana
It wasn't the fruit that laid her low
But the skin of the thing that made her go.

On a politician:
    For eternal salvation
    He received nomination,
    And as he expected,
    Was duly elected.

EPITAPHS

On a millionaire:
   He thought of course his holdings must
   Admit him to the Heavenly Trust—
   But when he handed in his proxy,
   He found they wanted orthodoxy.

Conjugal Epitaphs

In a Devonshire churchyard:
    Charity, wife of Gideon Bligh,
    Underneath this stone doth lie.
    Nought was she e'er known to do
    That her husband told her to.

Intended for his wife:
  Here lies my wife: here let her lie!
  Now she's at rest, and so am I.
        JOHN DRYDEN, 1631–1701.

Bayfield, Miss.:
  Here lies my wife in earthly mould,
  Who when she lived did naught but scold.
  Peace! wake her not, for now she's still,
  She had; but now I have my will.

A Welsh husband thus sings above the grave of his better-half:

This spot is the sweetest I've seen in my life,
For it raises my flowers and covers my wife.

Burlington, Vt.:

She lived with her husband fifty years
And died in the confident hope of a better life.

On a poet:

Here let a bard unenvied rest
Who no dull critic dare molest,
Escaped from the familiar ills,
Of thread-bare coat and unpaid bills;
From rough bum-bailiff's upstart duns,
From sneering pride's detested sons,
From all those pest'ring ills of life,
From, worst of all, a scolding wife.

Here lies my poor wife, much lamented
She's happy, and I'm contented.

The following appeared upon a wife's tomb:
>Husband, prepare to follow me!

In time the husband added this:
>I cannot come, my dearest life,
>For I have married another wife.
>And much as I would come to thee,
>I now must live and die with she.

On a bad wife, by her husband (from the Greek):
>Ah, once dear partner of my days,
>Willing to thee this tomb I raise;
>My grateful thoughts your shade pursue
>In this small gift so justly due.
>No envious tongue, with clamors rude
>Arraign'd this fact of gratitude,
>For all must know that with my wife
>I lost each hour of care and strife.

>Here lies John Dove who varied his life
>As a beater of gold by beating his wife.

A widower placed the following upon the tomb of a beloved wife:
>1890. The Light of my Life has gone out.
>1891. I have struck another match.

As father Adam first was fooled,
A case that's quite too common,
Here lies a man by a woman ruled,
The devil ruled the woman.

She was married twenty-six years and in all that time never once banged the door.

Within this grave do lie,
Back to back my wife and I.
When the last trump the air shall fill,
If she gets up I'll just lie still.

At Selby, Yorkshire:

Here lies my wife, a sad slattern and shrew,
If I said I regretted her, I should lie too!

Stowe, Vt.:

My wife from me departed
   And robbed me like a knave;
Which caused me broken hearted
   To sink into this grave.
My children took an active part,
   To doom me did contrive;
Which stuck a dagger in my heart
   That I could not survive.

Hollis, New Hampshire:

    Here lies Cynthia, Stevens' wife
    She lived six years in calms and strife.
    Death came at last and set her free.
    I was glad and so was she.

The following is copied from a country churchyard:

Here lies the body of JAMES ROBINSON, and RUTH his wife.
    "Their warfare is accomplished."

From St. Agnes, Cornwall:

    Here lies the body of Joan Carthew,
    Born at St. Columb, died at St. Cue;
    Children she had five,
    Three are dead, and two alive;
    Those that are dead choosing rather
    To die with their mother than live with
        their father.

From Painswick churchyard, near Stroud, Gloucestershire:

    'My wife is dead, and here she lies,
    Nobody laughs and nobody cries:
    Where she is gone to and how she fares,
    Nobody knows, and nobody cares.

At Acton, Gloucester:
    I laid my wife beneath this stone—for
        her repose
    And for my own.

    Here lies my poor wife
        Without bed or blanket,
    But dead as a door nail,
        And God be thankit.

Here lies the body of Mary Ford,
We hope her soul is with the Lord.
But if for Tophet she's changed this life,
Its better than being J. Ford's wife.

Burlington, Vermont:
Here lies the wife of brother Thomas,
Whom tyrant death has torn from us,
Her husband never shed a tear,
Until his wife was buried here.
And then he made a fearful rout,
For fear she might find her way out.

EPITAPHS

On a husband and wife:
They were so one, that none could say
Which of them ruled, or whether did obey —
He ruled because she would obey, and she
In so obeying, ruled as well as he.

Here lies the body of Roger Martin
She was a good wife to Roger, that's sartin.

On a wife who was a shrew:
    Resurgam—(I am risen.)
Underneath:
    "But don't tell my husband of it."

Essex, England:
    Here lies the man Richard,
      And Mary his wife,
   Whose surname was Prichard:
      They lived without strife;
    And the reason was plain,—
      They abounded in riches,
   They had no care nor pain,
      And his wife wore the breeches.

A man in New Hampshire having lost his wife, he caused a stone to be placed over the grave on which in the depth of his grief he ordered to be inscribed:

Tears cannot restore her—therefore I weep.

In Burlington churchyard, Mass.:
Sacred to the memory of Anthony Drake,
Who died for peace and quietness sake;
His wife was constantly scolding and scoffin',
So he sought for repose in a twelve-dollar coffin.

At Witchingham, on the tomb of THOMAS ALLEYN *and his* TWO WIVES, *ob.*, *1650:*
Death here advantage hath of life I spye,
One husband with two wives at once may lye.

As a beautiful example of what a good wife should be we offer in conclusion the following:

A monument in Streatham Church, Surrey, bears testimony to the virtues of

ELIZABETH, wife of Major Gen. Hamilton,
who was married near forty-seven years,
and
Never did one thing to disoblige her husband.
She died in 1746.

Rebecca, wife of William Lynne,
who died in 1663.

Might I ten thousand years enjoy my life,
I could not praise enough so good a wife.

Derogatory

Beneath this stone a lump of clay,
    Lies Arabella Young;
Who on the 24th of May,
    Began to hold her tongue.

Here lies the body of Sarah Sexton
She was a wife that never vexed one.
But I can't say as much for the one at the next stone.

Here lies, thank God, a woman who
Quarrelled and stormed her whole life through;
Tread gently o'er her mouldering form,
Or else you'll rouse another storm.

The following quaint epitaph is to be found in St. Giles's Cemetery collection:

>The mortal remains of
>JOHN BRINDELL,
>after an evil life of 64 years,
>Died June 18th, 1822,
>and lies at rest beneath this stone.
>Pause, reader; reflect;
>"Eternity, how surely thine."

On JOHN HILL, *Manchester, England:*

>Here lies JOHN HILL,
>A man of skill,
>Whose age was five times ten:
>He never did good
>And never would
>If he lived as long again.

On THOMAS KEMP, *who was hanged for sheep-stealing:*

>Here lies the body of THOMAS KEMP,
>Who lived by wool and died by hemp;
>There nothing would suffice the glutton
>But with the fleece to steal the mutton;
>Had he but worked and lived uprighter,
>He'd ne'er been hung for a sheep-biter.

On the tombstone of a disagreeable old man:
"Deeply regretted by all who never knew him."

On PARKER HALL, *who was born and executed at Oxford:*
Here lies Parker Hall, and what is more rarish,
He was born, bred, and hanged in St. Thomas's parish.

On MR. MILES. *From Webley churchyard, Yorks:*
This tombstone is a Milestone;
  Hah! how so?
Because beneath lies MILES who's
  MILES below.

On a tomb at Babraham in Cambridgeshire, bearing date 1600:
Here lyes Horatio Palavicene,
Who robb'd the Pope to lend the Queene.
He was a thief. A thief, thou ly'st:
For whie? He robbed but Antichrist.
Him Death with besom swept from Babram
Into the bosom of oulde Abram;
But then came Hercules with his club,
And struck him down to Beelzebub.

EPITAPHS

Here lies the body of Johnny Haskell,
A lying, thieving, cheating rascal;
He always lied, and now he lies,
He has no soul and cannot rise.

Here lies Dodge, who dodged all good
And dodged a deal of evil.
But after dodging all he could
He could not dodge the devil.

On a horse thief:

He found a rope and picked it up,
And with it walked away.
It happened that to other end
A horse was hitched, they say.
They took the rope and tied it up
Unto a hickory limb.
It happened that the other end
Was somehow hitched to him.

On a covetous person:

Of him within, nought e'er gratis was had,
That you read this so cheap now makes him sa

Here lies interred P. C. Bird
Who sang on earth till sixty-two.
Now up on high above the sky
No doubt he sings like sixty, too.

———

On a liar:
Here lies a man who while he lived
Was happy as a linnet.
He always lied while on the earth
And now he's lying in it.

———

Here lies the dust of the sinfullest wretch
That ever the devil delayed to fetch,
But the reader will grant it was needless he
    should
When he saw him a-coming as fast as he could.

———

Pinto lies here. 'Tis natural he should
Who lied through life as often as he could.
He thought of mending, but, to spite his will,
Death came unlooked for and bade him LIE STILL

———

From Lambeth churchyard, on WILLIAM
WILSON, *a quarrelsome Litigant:*
Here lieth W. W.
Who **never more** will trouble you, trouble you

Vicar Chest turned the bones of Martin, the regicide, out of the chancel of Chepstow Church, an act the vicar's son-in-law resented by inditing the following epitaph for him when he required one:

> Here lies at rest, I do protest,
> One Chest within another,
> The chest of wood was very good;
> Who says so of the other?

> Here lies a Cardinal who wrought
> Both good and evil in his time.
> The good he did was good for naught
> Not so the evil—that was prime.

Epitaph of Susan Blake:
(Written by Sir Thomas Moore at her urgent entreaty.)

> Good Susan Blake in royal state
> Arrived at last at Heaven's gate.

(After an absence of years and having fallen out with her he added these two lines:)

> But Peter met her with a club
> And knocked her back to Beelzebub.

On a worthless old maid:
  For three score years this life Cleora led,
At Morn she rose, at night she went to bed
                      W. COWPER.

On Sir Nathaniel Wraxall:
      Misplacing, mistaking,
      Misquoting, misdating
  Men, manners, things and facts all,
  Here lies Sir Nathan. Wraxall.
               G. COLMAN, *the younger.*

On a talkative old maid (1750):
  * Beneath this silent stone is laid
  A noisy antiquated maid,
  Who from her cradle talked till death,
  And ne'er before was out of breath.

  Here lies a most ingenuous youth,
  Who, when it suited, spake the truth;
  His parents' will he did obey,
  But always strove to have his way;
  Gentle as ever mother kissed,
  But every friend had felt his fist;
  His neighbor's ox he did not covet,
  But if he could he homeward druv' it.
  In short, the mandates of each table.
  He only broke when he was able.

John Calf was notoriously unpopular for, it i said, sufficient reasons. On his tomb are th words:

> Here lies John Calf,
> Thrice Mayor of Cork —
> Honor, Honor, Honor.

A local wag scribbled underneath:

O, cruel Death, more subtile than the fox,
That would not let this calf become an ox,
That with his fellows he might browse
    among the thorns,
And write his epitaph—Horns, Horns, Horns.

By Robert Burns

> In Seventeen hunder' an' forty-nine
> Satan took stuff to mak' a swine,
>   And cuist it in a corner;
> But wilily changed his plan,
> And shaped it something like a man,
>   And ca'ed it Andrew Turner.

Here lies Ned,
There is nothing more to be said —
Because we like to speak well of the dead.

Here lies one who was born and cried,
Told three score years and then he died,
His greatest actions that we find,
Were that he washed his hands and dined.

Beneath this smooth stone by the bone of his bone,
Sleeps master John Gill;
By lies when alive this attorney did thrive,
And now that he's dead he lies still.

Floyd has died and few have sobbed,
Since had he lived all had been robbed,
He's paid Dame Nature's debt 'tis said,
The only one he ever paid.
Some doubt that he resigned his breath,
Some vow he's cheated even Death.
If he is buried, then ye Dead, beware,
Look to your swaddlings, of your shrouds take care,
Lest Floyd to your coffin should make his way,
And steal your linen from your mouldering clay.

Here lie the bones of Foolish Fred,
Who wasted precious time in bed,
A nigger hit him on the head —
And thanks be praised—our Freddie's dead.
                                J. W.

Too bad for Heaven, too good for Hell,
So, where he's gone, I cannot tell.

Here lies John Racket
In his wooden jacket,
He kept neither horses nor mules;
   He lived like a hog,
   And died like a dog,
And left all his money to fools.

Here lieth the body of Martha Dias,
Always noisy, not very pious,
Who lived to the age of three score and ten,
And gave to worms what she refused to men.

Massachusetts:

  To the memory of Mary Gold,
 Who was gold in nothing but her name,
She was a tolerable woman for an acquaintance
But old Harry himself couldn't live with her.
   Her temper was furious
    Her tongue was vindictive
She resented a look and frowned at a smile,
   And was sour as vinegar.
She punished the earth upwards of 40 years,
  To say nothing of her relations.

John T—— Schoolmaster:

May he be punished as often as he punished us,
   He was a hard old shell.
  He said the Lord's Prayer every morning.
May the Lord forgive him as often as he forgave us.
  That was never.
We his scholars rear this stone over his ashes
   Though they are not worth it
  We are glad his reign is over.
        Amen.

In Horsley Down Church, Cumberland:

Here lie the bodies
of THOMAS BOND and MARY his wife
She was temperate, chaste, and charitable
BUT
She was proud, peevish and passionate.
She was an affectionate wife, and a tender mother
BUT
Her husband and her child whom she loved
Seldom saw her countenance without a disgusting frown,
Whilst she received visitors whom she despised with an endearing smile
Her behavior was discreet toward strangers
BUT
Independent to her family.
Abroad her conduct was influenced by good breeding
BUT
At home, by ill temper.
She was a professed enemy to flattery,
And was seldom known to praise or commend,
BUT
The talents in which she principally excelled,
Were difference of opinion and discovering flaws and imperfections.

She was an admirable economist,
And, with prodigality,
Dispensed plenty to every person in her family:
BUT
Would sacrifice their eyes to a farthing candle.
She sometimes made her husband happy with her
good qualities;
BUT
Much more frequently miserable—with her
many failings
Insomuch that in 30 years cohabitation he often
lamented
That maugre all her virtues,
He had not in the whole enjoyed two years
of matrimonial comfort,
AT LENGTH
Finding that she had lost the affection of her
husband
As well as the regard of her neighbours,
Family disputes having been divulged by
servants,
She died of vexation, July 20, 1768,
Aged 48 years.
Her worn-out husband survived her four months
and two days
And departed this life Nov. 28, 1768,
In the 54th year of his age.

WILLIAM BOND brother to the deceased erected
this stone
As a *weekly monitor,* to the surviving wives of this
parish
That they may avoid the infamy
of having their memories handed to posterity
With a PATCH WORK Character.

In Ostego County, N. Y.:
John burns.

Here lies the carcass
Of a cursed sinner,
Doomed to be roasted
For the Devil's dinner.

Ebenezer Dockwood
Aged forty-seven,
A miser and a hypocrite,
And never went to heaven.

On John Shaw, an attorney:

    Here lies John Shaw,
    Attorney-at-law,
    And when he died
    The Devil cried
    " Give us your paw,
    John Shaw,
    Attorney-at-law,
    Pshaw! Pshaw!"

Here lies the body of Robert Lowe
Whither he's gone I do not know.
If to the realms of peace and love
Farewell to happiness above.
If to a place of lower level
I don't congratulate the d——l.

This is to the memory of Ellen Hill,
A woman who would always have her will.
She snubbed her husband but she made good bread
Yet on the whole he's rather glad she's dead.
She whipped her children and she drank her gin,
Whipped virtue out and whipped the devil in.
May all such women go to some great fold
Where they through all eternity may scold.

England:

If heaven be pleased when sinners cease to sin,
If Hell be pleased when sinners enter in,
If earth be pleased when ridded of a knave,
Then all are pleased, for Coleman's in his grave.

Here lies old Caleb Ham,
  By trade a bum.
When he died the devil cried,
  Come, Caleb, come.

On a schoolmaster:

Here lie Willie Michie's bones;
  O Satan, when ye tak' him,
Gie him the schoolin' o' your weans,
  For clever deils he'll mak' em!

                R. BURNS.

On a suicide:

Earth'd up here lies an imp o' hell,
  Planted by Satan's dibble —
Poor silly wretch, he damns himsel
  To save the Lord the trouble.

                R. BURNS.

Here lies a mock marquis, whose titles were
    shamm'd,
If ever he rise—it will be to be damned.
R. BURNS.

On a miser:

Here lies one who for medicines would not give
    A little gold, and so his life he lost;
I fancy now he'd wish again to live,
    Could he but guess how much his funeral cost.

Another:

    The wretched man who moulders here
        Cared not for soul or body lost,
    But only wept when death drew near,
        To think how much his tomb would cost.

Another, from Falkirk, England:

    At rest beneath this slab of stone,
      Lies stingy Jimmy Wyett.
    He died one morning just at ten
      And saved a dinner by it.

Another:

>Here lieth Sparges
>Who died to save charges.

>Thin in beard and thick in purse,
> Never man beloved worse,
>He went to the grave with many a curse,
> The devil and he had both one nurse.

An old man's home in Seville, Spain, was founded in the seventeenth century by Don Miguel de Manara Bizentalo, a notorious profligate, who one night encountered a funeral procession when he was going home from a carousal. Inquiring who was dead, he heard his own name mentioned, and when he demanded sight of the corpse he beheld his own features. From that moment he was a changed man. He devoted himself and his entire fortune to works of mercy, and at his death founded this home for aged, friendless men, with an endowment that pays an income of $50,000 a year, making only one condition, which was that he should be buried under the threshold so that every one who entered should trample upon his grave, and that the following inscription should be engraved in letters large and plain enough for every one to read:

>Here repose the bones and ashes
>of the wickedest man in the world.
>God forgive him.
>Don Miguel Manara Bizentalo.
>Died 1664.

In Nova Scotia:
>Here lies old twenty-five per cent.
>The more he had the more he lent.
>The more he had the more he craved,
>Great God, can this poor soul be saved?

FRANCIS CHARTRES.
(*By Dr. Arbuthnot.*)
Here continueth to rot
The body of FRANCIS CHARTRES;
Who with an inflexible constancy,
and *inimitable uniformity* of life
persisted
In spite of *Age & Infirmities,*

In the practice of *every Human vice*,
excepting *Prodigality & Hypocrisy;*
His insatiable *Avarice* exempted him from the
first
His matchless *Impudence* from the second.
Nor was he more singular in the undeviating
pravity of his manners, than successful in
accumulating
Wealth
For without *Trade* or *Profession,*
Without *Trust of Public Money,*
And without *Bribe-Worthy Service,*
He acquired, or, more properly, created,
A Ministerial Estate
He was the only person of his time
Who could cheat without the mask of Honesty;
Retain his primeval Meanness when possessed of
Ten Thousand a Year;
And having daily deserved the Gibbet for what
he did,
Was at last condemned to it for what he could
not do.
O indignant reader!
Think not his life useless to mankind
Providence connived at his execrable designs.
To give to after ages a conspicuous Proof and
Example

EPITAPHS

small estimation is exorbitant wealth in
the sight of
God
bestowing it on the most unworthy of
ALL MORTALS.

Lie still, if you're wise,
You'll be damn'd if you rise.

Epitaphs on Occupations

A photographer:
>Here I lie, taken from life.

From Taibach Churchyard, South Wales:
>Hurrah! my boys, at the Parson's fall,
>For if he'd lived he'd a' buried us all.

Epitaph on a dentist:
>View this gravestone with gravity
>He is filling his last cavity.

>God works a wonder now and then,
>He, though a lawyer, was an honest man.

Sir John Strange.

This eminent barrister has the following epitaph:
>Here lies an honest lawyer —
>>that is Strange.

Another form of this idea :

Entombed within this vault a lawyer lies
Who, Fame assureth us was just and wise;
An able advocate and honest too;
That's wondrous strange, indeed, if it be true.

FOOTE, THE COMEDIAN.

FOOTE from his earthly stage, alas! is hurled:
Death took him off who took off all the world.

MRS. OLDFIELD (ACTRESS).

This we must own in justice to her shade,
'Tis the first bad exit OLDFIELD ever made.

On an author:

    Here lies an author—pray forgive
      The work that fed his pride;
    Long after death he thought to live,
      And long before it died.

Lord Brougham (for an orator):

  Here, reader, turn your weeping eyes,
    My fate a useful moral teaches;
  The hole in which my body lies
    Would not contain one-half my speeches.

On a philosopher, by Dibdin:

Here lies a philosopher knowing and brave,
　From whom Madam Nature ne'er hid the least wonder,
Who, looking to heaven, tumbled into his grave
　And disdain'd that same earth which he rotting lies under.

On a jockey:

　　Here lies John Michel Snider,
　　He was the fastest rider,
　　He won at every race,
　　At last he turned his face.

On an engine driver:

　I bid farewell to all the boys
　　Without a moment's notice.
　Death came to me while in my joys
　　Upon a locomotive.

On Barnum's fat woman:

　Grease, but living grease no more!

On a liquor-seller:

　　This is on me, boys!

On a chronic place-hunter:
Here lies John Baird in the only place for which he never applied.

On a tailor:
In life thy worth we never knew,
  We judged thee merely by thy clothes,
But at thy grave man stops to think
  How much to thee he really owes.

On a cannibal:
One who loved his fellow men, not wisely, but too well.

Here lies in the dust the mouldy old crust
  Of Nell Batcheldor, lately enclosen.
She well knew the arts of puddings and tarts
  And learned all the skill of the oven.
When she'd lived long enough, she made a last puff,
  A puff by her husband much praised,
Now here she doth lie to make a dirt pie
  In hopes that her crust may be raised.

Here lies a doctor destitute of drugs,
His soul has fled, his flesh is left for bugs.
He lived a life forever in the fault
And stops at last where all his patients halt.

On a faithful servant (from the French):

M. C. Zozimus lived thirty-eight years. A liberal master erected this monument to a faithful servant. He never spoke ill of any one; never did anything contrary to the will of his master; large sums of money were trusted continually to his care, from which he had not even the wish to take a single stiver for his own use.

On a coroner who hanged himself:
  He lived and died
  By *suicide*.

 Throughout his life he kneaded bread
  And deemed it quite a bore.
 But now six feet beneath earth's crust
  He needeth bread no more.

A bone collector:
   Here lies old Jones,
 Who all his life collected bones,
 Till death, that grim and bony spectre,
 That all-amassing bone collector,
 Boned old Jones, so neat and tidy,
 That here he lies all bona fide.

On Sir John Vanbrugh, architect:
  Under this stone, reader, survey
  Dead Sir John Vanbrugh's house of clay.
  Lie heavy on him, earth! for he
  Laid many heavy loads on thee.
              Dr. Abel Evans, *circa* 1700.

Over the grave of a Shropshire blacksmith:
  My sledge and anvil lie declined,
  My bellows too have lost their wind;
  My fire's extinct, my forge decay'd,
  And in the dust my body's laid:
  My coal is out, my iron's gone,
  My nails are drove, my work is done.

On an editor:
    "Here *lies* an Editor!
      Snooks, if you will;
    In mercy, Kind Providence,
      Let him *lie still!*
    He *lied* for his living: so
      He lived while he *lied:*
    When he could not *lie longer*
      He lied down and died."

On a pugilist, in Hanslope churchyard, near Wolverton:

    Strong and athletic was my frame
    Far away from home I came,
    And manly fought with Simon Byrnne
    Alas! but lived not to return.
    Reader, take warning by my fate,
    Unless you rue your case too late;
    And if you've ever fought before,
    Determine now to fight no more.

On an old woman who kept a pottery-shop in Chester, England:

    Beneath these stones lies old Kathering Gray,
    Changed from a busy life to lifeless clay;
    By earth and clay she got her pelf,
    But now is turned to earth herself.
    Ye weeping friends, let me advise,
    Abate your grief and dry your eyes,
    For what avails a flood of tears?
    Who knows but in a run of years,
    In some tall pitcher or bread pan,
    She in her shop may be again?

The following is copied from a Broomsgrove churchyard on a railway engineer who died in 1840:

 My engine now is cold and still,
 No water does my boiler fill;
 My coke affords its flame no more,
 My days of usefulness are o'er.
 My wheels deny their noted speed,
 No more my guiding hand they need;
 My whistle, too, has lost its tone,
 Its shrill and thrilling sounds are gone;
 My valves are now thrown open wide;
 My flanges all refuse to guide,
 My clacks also, though once so strong,
 Refuse to aid the busy throng:
 No more I feel each urging breath;
 My steam is now condensed in death,
 Life's railway o'er, each station passed,
 In death I'm stopped and rest at last.
 Farewell, dear friends, and cease to weep:
 In Christ I'm safe; in Him I sleep.

On a sailor, written by his messmate:
Here lies honest Jack, to the lobsters a prey,
Who liv'd like a sailor, free, hearty and gay;
His rigging well fitted, his sides close and tight,

His bread-room well furnished, his main-mast upright;
When Death, like a pirate, built solely for plunder,
Thus hailed honest Jack, in a voice loud as thunder:—
"Drop your peak, my old boy, and your topsails throw back,
For already too long you've remained on that tack."
Jack heard the dread call, and without more ado
His sails flattened in, and his bark she hove to.

Maryland (over the grave of a brave engineer):
    Until the brakes are turned on time,
    Life's throttle-valve shut down,
    He works to pilot in the crew
    That wears the martyr's crown
    On schedule time, on upper grade
    Along the homeward section,
    He lands his train in God's roundhouse
    The morn of resurrection.
    His time is full, no wages docked,
    His name on God's pay roll,
    And transportation through to Heaven
    A free pass for his soul.

Here lies a Doctor of Divinity,
Who was a Fellow, too, of Trinity.
He knew as much about Divinity
As other fellows do of Trinity.

Here lyeth a midwife brought to bed
    Deliveresse delivered.
Her body being churched here,
    Her soul gives thanks in yonder sphere.

On an embarrassed landholder:
Shed a tear for Simon Ruggle,
For life to him was a constant struggle,
He preferred the tomb and death's dark state,
To managing mortgaged real estate.

Conversational Epitaphs

Stowe, Vt.:
    My glass is run; yours is running.
    Remember death and judgment coming.

From a churchyard near London:
    Stop, reader! I have left a world,
      In which there was a world to do;
    Fretting and stewing to be rich —
      Just such a fool as you.

    Time was, I stood where thou dost now,
      And look'd, as thou look'st down on me;
    Time will be, thou shalt lie as low,
      And others then look down on thee.

On Stephen Rumbold, at Oxford:
    He lived one hundred and five,
      Sanguine and strong;
    An hundred to five
      You live not so long.

From a tombstone in Jersey:

"Reader, pass on!—don't waste your time
  O'er bad biography and bitter rhyme:
For what *I am* this crumbling clay ensures:
And what I was is no affair of yours.

In Bedlington churchyard, Durham:

Poems and epitaphs are but stuff :
Here lies ROBERT BURROWS, that's enough.

At Wing Church, Bucks:

Honest old THOMAS COTES, that sometimes was
Porter at Ascott Hall, hath now (alas!)
Left his key, lodge, fyre, friends, and all to have
A room in Heaven. This is that good man's
    grave,
Reader, prepare for thine, for none can tell,
But that you two may meet to-night. Farewell.
  He died 20th November, 1648.
  Set up at the appointment and charges of
      his Friend Geo. Hovghton.

Gridiwokag, 1635:

  ₓ Beneath this stone now dead to grief
  Lies Grid the famous Wokag chief.
  Pause here and think, you learned prig,
  This man was once an Indian big.
  Consider this, ye lowly one,
  This man was once a big in—jun.
  Now he lies here, you too must rot,
  As sure as pig shall go to pot.

1680.

Short was my stay in this vain world,
All but a seeming laughter,
Therefore mark well thy words and ways,
For thou com'st posting after.

From Shoreditch churchyard:

  We must all die, there is no doubt;
  Your glass is running—mine is out.

At Chichester:

  Art thou in health and spirits gay?
  I too was so the other day;
  And thought myself of life as safe
  As thou who readst my epitaph.

Upon C. C. B., aged 5 years, at Walcott, Norfolk:

    When the Archangel's trump shall blow,
      And souls to bodies join,
    Many will wish their lives below
      Had been as short as mine.

From a churchyard in Ireland:

    Here lies PAT STEELE.
      That's very true:
    Who was he? What was he?—
    What's that to you?

In Seven Oaks churchyard, Kent:

Grim Death took me without any warning
I was well at night, and died in the morning.

On a tomb in St. Pancras:

    GODFREY HILL, æt. 46.
—Thus far am I got on my journey;
    READER:
    Canst thou inform me
    What follows next?

Johnnie Dow's Epitaph:
    Wha lies here?
    I, Johnnie Dow.
    Hoo, Johnnie is that you?
    Ay, man, but I'm dead now.

Punning Epitaphs

On a celebrated cook:
>Pease to his hashes.
>(Peace to his ashes.)

Falkirk, England:
Here under this sod and under these trees
Is buried the body of Solomon Pease.
But here in his hole lies only his pod
His soul is shelled out and gone up to God.

>Here lies Matthew Mudd,
>Death did him no hurt;
>When alive he was *mud*,
>Now he's nothing but dirt.

On the EARL OF KILDARE:
>Who killed Kildare?
>Who dare Kildare to kill?
>Death killed Kildare,
>Who dare kill whom he will.

On a music master named STEPHEN:
STEPHEN and Time are now both even;
Stephen beat time, but now Time's beat STEPHEN.

At St. Giles, Cripplegate:
Under this marble fair
  Lies the body entomb'd of GERVAISE AIRE;
He dyd not of an ague fit,
  Nor surfeited by too much wit:
Methinks this was a wondrous death,
  That Aire should die for want of breath.

>Here lies Ann Mann.
> She lived an old maid
> But died an old Mann.

Boston (Granary Burying ground):

>Here I lie bereft of breath
>Because a cough carried me off;
>Then a coffin they carried me off in.

In Poole churchyard, on a tall man named DAY:

>As long as long can be,
>So long so long was he;
>How long, how long, dost say?
>As long as the longest DAY.

On MISS ELIZA MORE:

>Here lies one who never lied before,
>And one who never will lie More,
>To which there need be no more said.

Thomas All:

>Reader, beneath this marble lies
>ALL that was noble, good, and wise;
>ALL that once was formed on earth,
>ALL that was of mortal birth;
>ALL that liv'd above the ground,
>May within this grave be found:

If you have lost or great or small,
Come here and weep, for here lies ALL;
Then smile at death, enjoy your mirth,
Since God has took his ALL from earth.

On an organist at St. Mary, Winton College, Oxford:

MERIDITH

Here lies one blown out of breath,
Who lived a merry life, and died a Meridith.

On Mr. Peck:

Here lies a Peck which some men say
Was first of all a Peck of clay,
This wrought with skill divine, while fresh,
Became a curious Peck of flesh.
Through various forms its Maker ran,
Then adding breath made Peck a man,
Full fifty years Peck felt life's troubles,
Till death relieved a Peck of troubles,
Then fell poor Peck as all things must.
And here he lies—a Peck of dust.

On a man who was cremated:

The soul has flown
And the body's flue.

On a Mr. Partridge who died in May:

What! Kill a partridge
In the month of May,
Not quite sportsman-like,
Eh, Death, eh?

Bacchanalian

JOHN SCOTT, Brewer.
Poor John Scott is buried here
    Tho' once he was both hale and stout.
Death stretched him on his bitter bier,
    In another world he hops about.

Manchester, England:
Beneath these stones repose the bones of Theodosius Grimm.
    He took his beer from year to year
        And then the bier took him.

At Winchester:
Here sleeps in peace a Hampshire Grenadier,
    Who caught his death by drinking cold small beer.
Soldiers, be wise from his untimely fall,
    And, when ye're hot, drink strong or none at all.

In Hockheim churchyard:

This grave holds Caspar Schink, who came to dine,
And taste the noblest vintage of the Rhine;
Three nights he sat, and thirty bottles drank,
Then lifeless by the board of Bacchus sank:
One only comfort have we in the case —
The trump will raise him in the proper place.

In Thetford churchyard:

My grandfather lies buried here,
My cousin Jane, and two uncles dear;
My father perish'd with inflammation in the thighs,
And my sister drop't down dead in the Minories.
But the reason I'm here interr'd, according to my thinking,
Is owing to my good living and hard drinking;
If therefore, good Christians, you wish to live long,
Don't drink too much wine, brandy, gin, or anything strong.

Epitaphs on Infants and Children

In Islington churchyard over an infant, aged four months:
"Honor thy father and thy mother
   That thy days may be long in the land
   That the Lord thy God giveth thee."

In Cypress Hill cemetery, L. I., on a child:
"There is a special Providence
   In the fall of a sparrow."

Little Johnny Day lies here
   He neither fumes nor frets.
He had just reached his thirteenth year —
      Cigarettes.

JOHN ROSE,
Died Jan. 27, 1810,
Aged 10 years.

Dr Friends and companions all,
Pray warning take by me,
Don't venture on the ice too far
As 'twas the death of me.

Sacred to twins Charlie and Varlie
Sons of loving parents who died in infancy.

Here lie two infants by water confounded,
One died of dropsy, the other died drownded.

The pretty flowers that blossom here
Are fertilized by Gertie Greer.

Put away the little cradle,
   Soiled by little Tommy's thumb.
Put it in the garret corner
   Till another angel come.

LITTLE JIM
'He came to see the farce of life one day,
Tired of the first act, and so went away.

On an infant:
>   He tasted of life's bitter cup,
>   Refused to take the potion up,
>   Then turned his little head aside,
>   Disgusted with the taste, and died.

>   Here lies a babe that only cry'd
>   In baptism to be washed from sin, and dy'd.

New Milford, Conn. On a child drowned in a cistern:
>   In a moment he fled,
>   He ran to the cistern and raised the lid,
>   His father looked in, then did behold,
>   His child lay dead and cold.

>   Two lovelier babes ye nare did see
>   Than Providence did give to me,
>   But they was took with ague fits
>   And here they lie as dead as nits.

New Haven, Conn., on a babe four days old:
>   Since I was so very soon done for,
>   I wonder what I was begun for.

Stowe, Vt.:
　　Sacred to the memory of three twins.

From Massachusetts, where a sorrowing and pious parent inscribed the following two lines to the memory of his dead child:
　　We cannot have all things to please us,
　　Poor little Tommy's gone to Jesus.

A sympathetic reader mistaking the point of the lament, added the lines:
　　Cheer up, for all may yet be well,
　　Perhaps poor Tommy's gone to Hell.

From South Wales. In Vaynor churchyard, near Merthyr Tydvil:
　　　　Here lie the bodies of three
　　　　　　Children dear,
　　　　Two at Llanwono and
　　　　　　One here.

Under these stones lies three children dear;
Two are buried at Taunton and I lie here.

Bayfield, Miss.:
(On a child struck by lightning):
>Struck by thunder.

Stop dear parent cast your eye,
And here you see your children lie.
Though we are gone one day before,
You may be cold in a minute more.

Died, on the 14th inst., Henry Wilkins Glyn, aged 3 days and 7 hours. After a long and painful illness, which he bore with Christian fortitude, this youthful martyr departed to his rest.

From Portland, Oregon:
>Beneath this stone our baby lies,
>   It neither cries nor hollers,
>It lived but one and twenty days,
>   And cost us forty dollars.

Portland, Oregon:
>The little hero that lies here
>   Was conquered by the diarrhœa.

From Germantown, Pa.:
>Here lies the bones of my boy Fritz,
>The Lord killed him with ague fits.
>He was too good to live with me,
>So He took him home to live with He.

On a dead infant:
>She never told her love.

Brief Epitaphs

On an author:
FINIS.

On a fellow of the Oxford University:
PRÆIVIT.
(*He is gone before.*)

On a painter:
Here lies a *finished* artist.

Laconic:
Snug.

In Seven Oaks churchyard, Kent, on a lady whose initials were E. S. T.:
E. S. T., sed non est!

On an Angler:
Hook'd it.

On RICHARD GROOMBRIDGE, *in Horsham churchyard:*

   He was.

On a Miser, by W. F.:
   Gone underground.

On a well-known Shakespearian actor:
   ✗ EXIT Burbage.

On Dr. Fuller, the Celebrated Divine:
   ✓ Here lies Fuller's Earth.

   Fui.
   (I was.)

Cardinal Onumphiro, at Rome:
  Here lies a shadow—ashes—nothing.

An Italian Inscription:
   I was well,
   I would be better,
   And here I am.

Another Italian Epitaph:
>Lelio is buried here.
>He was born.   He lived.   He died.

Dr. Caius, founder of Caius College:
>Fui Caius.   (I was Caius.)

An Irish Epitaph of commendable brevity:
>Finis
>Maginnis.

The following was proposed for Lord Camden, the title of his chief book:
>Camden's Remains.

On an auctioneer at Greenwood:
>Going, Going, Gone.

At Augusta, Maine:
>After life's Scarlet Fever
>I sleep well.

For a work-house pauper was suggested:
>Thomas Thorpse,
his corpse.

But an indignant and economical board of directors changed it to

Thorpse
corpse.

On Dr. Walker, author of "Walker's Particles":

> Here lie Walker's Particles.

TASSO.

The only epitaph placed on Tasso's tomb was:
Ossa Tassi
(The bones of Tasso.)

COUNT TESSIN.

On the tomb of Count Tessin, Governor of Gustavus III of Sweden, written by himself:
Tandem Felix.
(Happy at last.)

A brief one:
Miserrimus.

Pathetic Epitaphs

Pembroke, Mass.:

Here lies a poor woman who always was tired,
She lived in a house where help wasn't hired.
The last words she said were "Dear friends, I am going,
Where washing ain't wanted, nor mending, nor sewing.
There all things is done just exact to my wishes,
For where folk don't eat there's no washing of dishes.
In Heaven loud anthems forever are ringing,
But having no voice, I'll keep clear of the singing.
Don't mourn for me now, don't mourn for me never;
I'm going to do nothing forever and ever."

On a lover who was dumb (from the French:)
    This is a lover's early tomb
    Who died while yet in beauty's bloom.
    Iris for him drops many a tear;
    Her grief I'm sure must be sincere,
    For none, of all her am'rous train,
    Was half so secret as this swain.

From Grace churchyard, Jamaica, Long Island:
    1780.
Eternal bliss shall innocence enjoy
And endless pleasures which can never cloy.
While here entombed a virtuous youth doth
    rest
In certain hopes of being completely blest.

    1749.
Into Thy Courts, O Lord, she's fled,
Through the dark mansions of the dead.
Within Thy Palace now she's fixed
In joys celestial and unmixed.

In Cheraw churchyard, South Carolina:

    My name, my country,
      What are they to thee?
    What, whether high or low,
      My pedigree?
    Perhaps I far surpassed
      All other men:
    Perhaps I fall below them all;
      What then?
    Suffice it, stranger,
    Thou see'st a tomb,
    Thou know'st its use;
    It hides—no matter whom.

Rich born, rich bred, yet Fate adverse
His wealth and fortune did reverse.
He lived and died immensely poor
July the tenth aged ninety-four.

In the churchyard at Hammersfield, Suffolk, on ROBERT CRYTOFT, *ob. 1810, æt. 90:*

As I walk'd by myself, I talk'd to myself,
    And thus myself said to me:
Look to thyself, and take care of thyself,
    For nobody cares for thee.

So I turn'd to myself, and I answered myself,
  In the self-same reverie:
Look to myself, or look not to myself,
  The self-same thing will it be.

A bachelor's epitaph:

At threescore winters' end I died,
A cheerless being, sole and sad,
The nuptial knot I never tied —
And wish my father never had.

Another variant:

I Dionysius underneath this tomb
Some sixty years of age have reached my doom.
Ne'er having married, think it sad,
And I wish my father never had.

In Llangollan Churchyard, Wales:

Our life is but a summer's day:
Some only breakfast, and away;
Others to dinner stay and are full fed;
The oldest man but sups and goes to bed.
Large his account who lingers out the day;
Who goes the soonest has the least to pay.

At length, my friends, the feast of life is o'er.
I've eat sufficient and I'll drink no more,
My night is come, I've spent a jovial day,
'Tis time to part, but O what is to pay?

I crossed the seas till I was tired,
To find some port I long desired.
From rocks and shoals this place seems clear
So I in peace have anchored here.

She died, poor dear, of disappointed love,
And angels bore her soul to realms above.
When her young man is summoned, so they say,
He will be carried off the other way.

He's left this world where griefs abound —
　This world so cold and drear —
For t'other one. We hope he's found
　A warmer welcome there.

All you that told lies of my mother and me,
Come to my grave and see.

Nov. 3, 1702. Aged 88 years.

Here lies the body of Walter Welch, son of Michael Welch of Great Shelsley, who left him a fine estate in Shelsley, Hartlebury, and Arley; who was ruined by three Quakers, three lawyers, and a fanatick to help them.

At Lebanon, Conn.:

    As a stranger she did die,
    In strange lands she doth lie.
    Here by strangers she was laid,
    And her funeral charges paid.

In Calvary cemetery, Chicago:

    In memory of
    John S——
    who
    departed this life
    Jan. 13, 1859. Aged 28 years.
Cold is my bed, but oh, I love it,
For colder are my friends above it.

In St. Michael's churchyard, Workington:
1808.
You villains! if this stone you see,
Remember that you murdered me!
You bruised my head, and pierced my heart,
Also my bowels did suffer part.

Our papa dear has gone to Heaven
To make arrangements for eleven.

Stowe, Vt.:
Here lies the body of old Uncle David,
Who died in the hope of being sa-ved.
Where he's gone or how he fares,
Nobody knows and nobody cares.

Here lies Sir JOHN GUISE:
No one laughs, no one cries:
Where he's gone, and how he fares,
No one knows, and no one cares.

Hollis, New Hampshire:

> Here the old man lies
> No one laughs and no one cries
> Where he's gone or how he fares
> No one knows and no one cares.
> But his brother James and his wife Emeline
> They were his friends all the time.

On a tombstone without a name:

Ye passers-by, stay not to ask what's my name,
I'm nothing at present, from nothing I came;
I never was much, and am now less than ever:
And idle hath certainly been his endeavour,
Who, coming from nothing, to nothing is fled,
Yet thought he might something become were he
    dead.

Epitaphs of Celebrated Persons

The epitaphs of many men of true greatness are distinguished for their brevity and simplicity, in striking contrast to the fulsome self-adulation of many celebrities of the second class.

PLATO.

Plato's epitaph by Speusippus is here given:
PLATO's dead form this earthly shroud invests:
His soul among the godlike heroes rests.

DARWIN.

The epitaph of this great student of Nature, taken from Westminster Abbey, is as simple and unpretentious as was his life:

CHARLES ROBERT DARWIN
Born 12 February, 1809.
Died 19 April, 1882.

Faraday.

In Highgate cemetery is the following strikingly simple inscription:

MICHAEL FARADAY
Born 22nd September, 1791;
Died 25th August
1867.

Alexander the Great.

"Sufficit huic tumulus
Cui non sufficeret obis."

"Here a mound suffices for one for whom the world was not large enough."

By Simonides, on the death of TIMOCREON, *translated by* MERIVALE:

After much eating, drinking, lying and slandering
TIMOCREON of Rhodes here rests from wandering.

Shakespeare.

The following lines, said to have been written by Shakespeare, are inscribed on a flat stone which marks the spot where he is buried in the churchyard of Stratford-on-Avon:

    Good friend, for Jesu's sake forbeare
      To dig the dust enclosed here;
    Blessed be he that spares these stones,
      And curst be he that moves my bones.

The last great English poet was laid to rest near the dust of his fellow-bards; the following marks the spot:

    Robert
    Browning
    1889.

Over the grave of the author of "Little Nell," in Westminster Abbey, is the following simple inscription:

    Charles Dickens
    Born 7th February, 1812;
    Died 9th June, 1870.

The following from Westminster Abbey, on John Gay, the Poet, is said to have been written by himself:

> Life is a jest, and all things show it;
> I thought so once and now I know it.
> 1688–1732.

On Oliver Goldsmith:

> Here lies Nolly Goldsmith, for shortness called Noll,
> Who wrote like an angel, but talked like poor Poll.
> DAVID GARRICK, 1716–1779.

For one (himself) who would not be buried in Westminster Abbey:

> Heroes and kings, your distance keep;
> In peace let one poor poet sleep,
> Who never flattered folks like you;
> Let Horace blush, and Virgil too.

SIR CHRISTOPHER WREN.

Visitors to St. Paul's Cathedral, of which, as is so well known, Sir Christopher was the architect, will see over the north door the following lines:

> Si monumentum quæris, circumspice.
> (*If his monument you seek, look around.*)

In Eton College Sir Henry Wotton has the following curious epitaph, in Latin, inscribed above his grave :

Here lies the author of this sentence :
An itching for dispute is the scab of the church.
Seek his name elsewhere.

ROBIN HOOD.

Hear undernead this latil stean
Laiz Robert Earl of Huntingdon,
Nea arcir ver az hie sa geud,
An pipil kauld him Robin Heud.
Sich atlaz az he an iz men
Vil England nior si agen.
Obit 25 Kalend, Dikimbris, 1247.

In Bunhill Fields a popular author was buried, and the following is his epitaph:

DANIEL DE-FOE
Born 1661
Died 1731.
Author of
Robinson Crusoe.
This monument is the result of an appeal,
in the "Christian World" newspaper

to the boys and girls of England, for funds
to place a suitable memorial upon the grave
of
DANIEL DE-FOE.
It represents the united contributions
of seventeen hundred persons
Septr. 1870.

John Bunyan was also buried in Bunhill Fields. His tomb bears the following:

JOHN BUNYAN
Author of the
Pilgrim's Progress
Obt 31st Augt, 1688
Æt. 60.

On the other side of the tomb we read as follows:

Restored by public
Subscription under the
Presidency of the Right
Honorable the Earl
of Shaftesbury. May
1862.
JOHN HIRST, Hon. Sec.

On H. R. H. Frederick, Prince of Wales, died March 26, 1751:

    Here lies Fred,
      Who was alive, and is dead.
    Had it been his father
      I had much rather;
    Had it been his mother,
      Better than another;
    Had it been his sister,
      No one would have missed her;
    Had it been his entire generation,
      So much the better for the nation;
    But since 'tis only Fred,
      Who was alive, and is dead,
    There's no more to be said.

In St. Anne's churchyard, Soho:
(On Theodore, last King of Corsica, who died Dec. 11, 1756, shortly after his liberation from the King's Bench Prison, and is buried in the churchyard of St. Anne's, Westminster.)

    Near this place is interred
    Theodore, King of Corsica;
  Who died in this parish Dec. 11,
        1756
    immediately after leaving

the King's Bench Prison,
by the benefit of the Act of Insolvency;
In consequence of which
he registered the kingdom of Corsica
for the use of his creditors.

The grave, great teacher, to a level brings
Heroes and beggars, galley slaves and kings,
But Theodore this moral learn'd ere dead:
Fate pour'd its lesson on his living head,
Bestow'd a kingdom, but deny'd him bread.
HORACE WALPOLE, 1717-1797.

THE DUKE OF WELLINGTON.

On the magnificent sarcophagus erected to the memory of the Iron Duke in St. Paul's Cathedral is the simple inscription:

ARTHUR, FIRST DUKE OF WELLINGTON.

Around the base which supports the pillars of the canopy, are the names of the battles which the Duke fought:

North Side.—Vittoria, Bayonne, Toulouse, Nive, Peronne, Orthes, Waterloo, Quetrebras, Nivelle, Adour, Salamanca, Pampeluna, Bidassoa, Badajos.

East Side.—Fuentes-d-onor, Morales, Sarugal, Fons-d-aronce, Arreyo-Molino, Aldea-Da-Ponte, Tormes, Homaza, Ciudad-Rodrigo.
South Side.—Talavera, Busaco, Kioge, Vimiero, Zubiri, Argaum, Gawilghur, Assaye, Ahmeb-nugger, Conagul, Bulos, Rolica, El-Bodon, Almeida, Douro.
West Side.—San-Sebastian, Roncesvalles, Aretsou, Elretiro, Burgos, Canal-Nuova, Camzal, Ponte-Ciberte, Torres-Vedras.

———

Elihu Yale, the founder of Yale College at New Haven, lies buried in Wrenham, Wales. His monument bears this inscription:

Born in America, in Europe bred
In Africa traveled, in Asia wed,
Where long he lived and thrived
And at London died.
Much good, some ill he did so hope all's even
And his soul through mercy is gone to Heaven.
You that survive and read this tale take care,
For this most certain event to prepare;
Where blest in peace the actions of the just
Smell sweet and blossom in the silent dust.

Robert Louis Stevenson's epitaph, written by himself:

> Under the wide and starry sky
> Dig the grave and let me lie.
> Glad did I live and gladly die
> And I laid me down with a will.
> This be the verse you grave for me:
> "Here he lies where he longed to be.
> Home is the sailor, home from the sea,
> And the hunter, home from the hill."

On Robert Burton, author of "The Anatomy of Melancholy":

> Here lies the body of Democritus Junior,
> Who lived and died by melancholy.

> Here lies John Duke of Marlborough
> Who run the French thorough and thorough.
> He marry'd Sarah Jennings, spinster,
> Dy'd at St. James, bury'd at Westminster.

George Washington.

At Mt. Vernon, on the sarcophagus of the "Father of his Country," it is a matter of regret to all who read the inscription to find it also an advertisement:

> Washington.
> By the permission of
> Lawrence Lewis
> The surviving executor of
> George Washington,
> this sarcophagus
> was presented by
> John Struthers,
> of Philadelphia, Marble Mason,
> A. D., 1837.

Thomas Jefferson.

At Monticello, Va.:
> Here lies buried
> Thomas Jefferson,
> author of the Declaration of American
> Independence,
> Of the Statute of Virginia for Religious Freedom,
> And Father of the University of Virginia.

Benjamin Franklin.

At 5th and Arch Streets, Philadelphia:

Benjamin
and } Franklin.
Deborah

At the age of twenty-three, while a journeyman printer, Franklin wrote for himself this epitaph, which for some reason was not placed upon his tomb:

The body of
B. Franklin
Printer
Like the cover of an old book,
its contents torn out,
and stripped of its lettering and gilding,
lies here, food for worms.
But the work shall not be wholly lost;
for it will, as he believed, appear once more,
in a new and more perfect addition,
corrected and amended
by the Author.
He was born Jan. 6, 1706.
Died   17

At Newport, R. I., on Commodore Perry:
Oliver Hazard Perry:
At the age of 27
he achieved the victory of
Lake Erie,
Sept. 10, 1813.
Erected by the city of
Newport.

On Daniel Webster:
Born Jan. 18th, 1782.
Died Oct. 24th, 1852.
"The Gospel "—" a divine reality."

WOLFE AND MONTCALM.

On a monument in Palace Garden, Quebec, Canada, erected to the memory of the two generals, is a Latin inscription, the translation of which is:

Wolfe—Montcalm.
Military virtue gave them a common death.
History a common fame.
Posterity a common monument.

Yazoo City, Miss.:
>Here lie two grandsons of
John Hancock, first signer of the
Declaration of Independence.
(Their names are respectively Geo. M.
and John H. Hancock)
and their eminence hangs on
their having had a grandfather.

General Wm. T. Sherman.
St. Louis, Mo.:
>William Tecumseh Sherman,
General, U. S. A.,
Born at Lancaster, O.
Feb. 8, 1820,
Died at New York city,
Feb. 14, 1891.
Faithful and Honorable.

On General Robert E. Lee. By Philip S Worssley:
>An angel's heart, an angel's mouth,
> Not Homer's, could alone for me
>Hymn well the great Confederate South,
> Virginia first, and Lee!

HENRY CLAY.

Inscription on gold medal, struck in commemoration of Henry Clay by his friends:

Senate, 1806.
Speaker, 1811.
War of 1812 with Great Britain.
Ghent, 1814.
Spanish America, 1822.
Missouri Compromise, 1821.
America System, 1824.
Greece, 1824.
Secretary of State, 1825.
Panama Instructions, 1826
Tariff Compromise, 1833.
Public Domain, 1833–1841.
Peace with France Preserved, 1835.
Compromise, 1850.

Alexander Hamilton, at Wehock, N. J.:

On this spot fell 11 July, 1804, in the 47 year of his age, Major General Alexander Hamilton.

As an expression of their profound respect for his memory, and their unfeigned grief for his loss, the St. Andrews Society of the State of New York, have erected this monument.

(Another monument and inscription on Hamilton is to be found in New York city, erected by the corporation of Trinity Church.)

STEPHEN A. DOUGLASS.

Chicago, Ill.:
Judge Douglass.
Born April 23d, 1813—died June 3d, 1866.
"Tell my children to obey the laws and uphold the constitution."

ABRAHAM LINCOLN.

From the head of the sarcophagus of Abraham Lincoln in Oak Ridge Cemetery, Springfield, Ill. :
"With malice toward none."
Lincoln.
"With Charity to all."

On the exterior of the monument in letters a foot high, thirty feet above the ground, is the single word
Lincoln.

The only other words on the monument are the names of the States.

Miscellaneous Epitaphs

From Bunhill Fields burying-ground:
Here lies
DAME MARY PAGE
Relict of Sir Gregory Page, Bart.
She departed this life
March 4th, 1728,
in the 56th year of her age.
In 67 months she was tapped 66 times. Had taken away 240 gallons of water, without ever repining at her case, or even fearing the operation.

Winslow, Maine:
Here Betsy Brown her body lies.
Her soul is flying in the skies.
While here on earth she ofttimes spun
Six hundred skeins from sun to sun,
And wove one day, her daughter brags,
Two hundred pounds of carpet rags.

From Hyden churchyard, Yorks:
Here lies the body of
WILLIAM STRATTON, of Paddington,
buried 18th day of May, 1734, aged 97 years;
who had by his first wife 28 children;
by his second 17; was own father to 45;
grandfather to 86; greatgrandfather to 23.
In all 154 children.

Chelsea:
Agreeable to the memory of
Mrs. Alinda Tewksbury.
She was not a believer in the Christian idolitry.

Beneath this monumental stone
Lies half a ton of flesh and bone.

Here lies Jane Smith,
Wife of Thomas Smith, Marble Cutter
This monument was erected by her
husband as a tribute to her memory
and a specimen of his work.
Monuments of this same style are
two hundred and fifty dollars.

On Susan Mum:
>To the memory of SUSAN MUM
>Silence is wisdom.

In Luton Church:
>Here lies the body of Thomas Proctor,
>Who lived and died without a doctor.

From a tombstone near Williamsport, Penn.:
>Sacred to the Memory of
>HENRY HARRIS,
>Born June 27th, 1821, of Henry Harris
>And Jane his Wife.
>Died on the 4th of May, 1837, by the kick of a colt in his bowels.
>
>Peaceable and quiet, a friend to his father and mother, and respected by all who knew him, and went to the world where horses don't kick, where sorrow and weeping is no more.

On WILLIAM BECK :
>Here lies the body of WILLIAM BECK,
>He was thrown at a hunt and broke his neck.

The celebrated Daniel Lambert's epitaph, St. Martin's, Stamford Baron, England:

Altus in animo, in corpore maximus.

In remembrance of that prodigy in Nature,

DANIEL LAMBERT.

A native of Leicester, who was possessed of an exalted, convivial mind;
and in personal greatness had no competitor;
He measured 3 ft. 1 in. round the legs, 9 ft. 4 in. round the body, and weighed 52 st. 11 lb.
He departed this life on the 21st June, 1809,
Aged 39 years.

As a testimony of respect, this stone is erected by his friends in Leicester.

From West Grinstead churchyard, Sussex:
Vast strong was I, but yet did dye,
And in my grave asleep I lye
My grave is stean'd round about.
Yet I hope the Lord will find me out.

The following is copied from an old tombstone in Scotland:

Here lies the body of Alexander Macpherson,
He was a very extraordinary person:
He was two yards high in his stocking-feet,
And kept his accoutrements clean and neat.
He was slew
At the battle of Waterloo:
He was shot be a bullet
Plumb through his gullet:
It went in at his throat
And came out at the back of his coat.

From an ancient Scottish epitaph:

John Carnagie lies here,
   Descended from Adam and Eve;
If any can boast of a pedigree higher,
   He will willingly give them leave

In a churchyard near Boston, Mass.:

Of pneumonia supervening consumption,
complicated with other diseases, the
main symptoms of which was insanity.

In Monument Cemetery, Philadelphia:
Our first deposit in Heaven.

Huntington, West Va.:
"Here lies the body of J. Wesley Webb, a firm believer in the Lord Jesus Christ, Jeffersonian Democracy and the M. E. Church."

Elizabeth L. H. (by Ben Johnson):
  Would'st thou hear what man say
  In a little? Reader, stay:
  Underneath this stone doth lie
  As much beauty as could die;
  Which in life did harbour give
  To more virtue than doth live.
  If at all she had a fault,
  Leave it buried in this vault.
  One name was Elizabeth,
  The other, let it sleep with death;
  Fitter, where it died to tell,
  Than that it lived at all. Farewell.

From the Old Men's Hospital, Norwich:
⁄ In memory of
MRS. PHEBE CREWE
Who died May 28, 1817,
Aged 77 years.
Who during forty years
practice as a midwife
in this City, brought into
the world nine thousand,
seven hundred and
thirty children.

(Lord Byron's epitaph on his Newfoundland dog at Newstead):
"To mark a friend's remains
These stones arise.
I never knew but one
And here he lies."

In Bickenhill Churchyard is a curious epitaph, evidently the work of some rustic mason who did not understand numeration, or else MRS. ANNIE SMITH was a very aged spinster indeed:

Here lyeth the BOdy of Mrs. ANIIE SMITH,
WhO dePartcd thiS Life OCtO the 28, in the
yeare 1701.
Shee LiVed a Maid And died aged 708.

From Wolstanton, on Anne Jennings:
Some have children, some have none;
Here lies the mother of twenty-one.

Spain:
Here lies John Quebecca
precentor to My Lord the King.
When he is admitted to the choir of angels whose society he will embellish and where he will distinguish himself by his powers of song—God shall say to the angels—
Cease, ye calves! and let me hear
John Quebecca, the precentor of
My Lord the King.

From Aberconway churchyard, Cærnarvonshire:
Here lieth the body of
NICHOLAS HOOKS, of Conway, gent.,
who was
the *one-and-fortieth child* of his father,
William Hooks, Esq., by Alice his wife,
and *the father of seven-and-twenty children;*
he died the 20th day of March, 1637.

In Doncaster churchyard:
Here lies 2 brothers by misfortun serounded,
One dy'd of his wounds, and the other was drownded.

In a Wiltshire churchyard:
Beneath this steane lyes our deare child who's gone from
  We
For evermore unto eternity;
Where, us do hope, that we shall go to *He*,
But Him can ne'er come back again to *We*.

In the year 1743, a monument was erected by subscription, in Bolton Churchyard, to the memory of Jenkins; it consists of a square base of freestone, four feet four inches on each side, by four feet six inches in height, surmounted by a pyramid eleven feet high. On the east side is inscribed:

This monument was
erected by contribution,
in ye year 1743 to ye memory
of Henry Jenkins.

On the west side:
Henry Jenkins.
Aged 169

In the church on a mural tablet of black marble, is inscribed the following epitaph, composed by Thomas Chapman, Master of Magdalen College, Cambridge:

Blush not, marble,
to rescue from oblivion
the memory of
HENRY JENKINS:
a person obscure in birth,
but of a life truly memorable;
for
he was enriched
with the goods of nature,
if not of fortune,
and happy
in the duration,
if not variety,
of his enjoyments;
and
tho' the partial world
despised and disregarded
his low and humble state,
the equal eye of Providence
beheld and blessed it
with a patriarch's health and length of days;
to teach mistaken man,

these blessings were entailed in temperance,
or, a life of labour and a mind at ease.
He lived to the amazing age of 169;
was interred here, Dec. 6th, (or 9), 1670,
and had this justice done to his memory 1743.

A wood-cutter at Ockham, Surrey:

The Lord saw good; I was lopping off wood,
 And down fell from the tree;
I met with a check, and I broke my neck,
 And so Death lopped off me.

On a young nobleman:

Children are snatched away sometimes,
To punish parents for their crimes:
Thy mother's merit was so great,
Heaven hastened thy untimely fate,
To make her character complete;
Though many virtues fill'd her breast,
'Twas resignation crowned the rest.

In Kensington churchyard:

Here are deposited the remains of
MRS. ANNE FLOYER,
the beloved wife of Mr. Richard Floyer,
of Thistle Grove, in this parish.
Died on Thursday, the 8th of May, 1823.
God hath chosen her as a pattern for the other Angels.

Orange County, N. Y.:

He was a man of invention great
Above all who he lived nigh;
But he could not invent to live
When God called him to die.

At. St. Albans:

Sacred to the memory of Miss Martha Gwynn,
Who was so very pure within,
She burst the outer shell of sin,
And hatched herself a cherubim.

At Toddington, Bedfordshire, on MARIA WENTWORTH, *who died in the year 1632, aged 18:*

 And here the pretiovs dyste is layde,
 Whose pverile tempered clay was made
 So fine, that it the gvest betray'd.

 Else the sovle grew so fast within,
 It broke the outer shell of sinne,
 And so was hatched a cherebim.

 In height it soar'd to God above,
 In depth it did to knowledge move,
 And spread in breadth, in general love.

 Before a pios dvtye shin'd,
 To parents, cvrtesie, behind;
 On either side an eqval mind.

 Good to the poore, to kindred dear,
 To servants kind, to friendship clear,
 To nothing but herself severe.

 Soe, though a virgin, yet a bride
 To everie grace, she jvstified
 A chaste poligamie, and dyed.

Under this yew tree
Buried would he be
Because his father—he
Planted this yew tree.

In Exeter Cathedral:
Here lies the Body of Captain Tully,
Aged an hundred and nine years fully;
And threescore years before, as Mayor,
The sword of this city he did bear;
Nine of his wives do with him lie,
So shall the tenth when she doth die.

Aberdeen, Scotland:
Here lies Martin Elmerod.
Have mercy on my soul, good God
As I would do were I Lord God
And you were Martin Elmerod.

Cornwall:
Forty-nine years they lived as man and wife,
And what's more rare, thus many without strife;
She first departing, he a few weeks tried
To live without her, could not, and so died.
Both in their wedlock's great Sabbatic rest
To be where there's no wedlock was blest,
And having here a jubilee begun
They're taken hence that it may ne'er be done.

On Robert Trollop, Architect, in Gateshead churchyard, Durham:

> Here lies Robert Trollop
> Who made yon stones roll up;
> When Death took his soul up,
> His body fill'd this hole up.

From a churchyard at Creltow, Salop:

> On a Thursday she was born,
> On a Thursday made a bride,
> On a Thursday put to bed,
> On a Thursday broke her leg, and
> On a Thursday died.

In a churchyard in the neighborhood of Oxford, on a Doctor of Divinity:

> He died of a quinsy,
> And was buried at Binsy.

From Kingston churchyard, in Hampshire:

> Live well—Die never
> Die well—Live for ever.

Westfield, New Jersey:
The dame that rests beneath this tomb
Had Rachel's beauty, Leah's fruitful womb,
Abigail's wisdom, Lydia's faithful heart,
Martha's just care, and Mary's better part.

In Durness churchyard, Sutherlandshire:
   Here doth lye the bodie
   Of John Flye, who did die
   By a stroke from a sky-rocket
   Which hit him on the eye-socket.

   Mammy and I together lived
     Just two years and a half;
   She went first—I followed next,
   The cow before the calf.

From Wrexham Church:
   Here lies interr'd beneath these stones
   The beard, the flesh, and eke ye bones
   Of Wrexham's clerk, old DANIEL JONES

In Kingston churchyard:

    Against his will
    Here lies George Hill,
    Who from a cliff
    Fell down quite stiff.

In Silton, Dorsetshire:

    Here lies a piece of Christ —
      A star in dust,
    A vein of gold—a china dish,
      That must
    Be used in Heaven when God
      Shall feed the just.

    Death loves a shining mark
          and
    In this case he had it.

Wiltshire, England:

    Beneath this stone in hope of Zion
    Is laid the landlord of the Lion,
    Resigned unto the Heavenly will
    His son keeps on the business still.

On a skeptic:
>I was not
>I am not
>I grieve not.

Another on a skeptic:
>Traveller, pass not by this inscription, but stand, and hear, and learn something before you pass on.
>
>There is no boat the Hades, no boatman Charon, no dog Cerberus, but all the dead are bones and dust, and nothing else.

The oldest epitaph in English is found in a churchyard in Oxfordshire, year 1370. Rendered into modern English it is:
>Man come and see how all dead shall be
>When you come poor and bare,
>Nothing have when we away fare
>All is weariness that we for care.

A Roman Warning, (translation):
I give to the Gods below this tomb to keep,
To Pluto, and to Demeter, and to Persephone,
And the Erinnyes, and all the Gods below.

If any one shall disfigure this sepulchre,
Or shall open it, or move anything from it,
To him let there be no Earth to walk, no sea to
  sail,
But may he be rooted out with all his race.

May he feel all diseases, shuddering and fever,
And madness, and whatsoever ills exist for beast
Or men, may these light on him who dares move
Aught from this tomb.

———

At Athens, (translation):
If there ever was a thoroughly good woman
I am she, both in reference to righteousness
And in all other ways.
But being such, I got no just return,
Neither from those from whom I expected it,
Nor from Providence.
Unhappy, I lie apart from my mother and father.
I say nothing about what gratitude they showed
  me.
Not they, but my sons provided for me.

In Luneburg, Hanover, Germany, a ham is preserved with the following inscription in gilt letters on a black marble slab:

Passer by contemplate here the mortal remains of
THE PIG
which acquired for itself imperishable glory,
by the discovery of the Salt Springs of Lune burg.

Qualis Vita,
Finis Ita.
(As he lived, so he died.)

From Wingfield, Suffolk:
Pope boldly says (some think the maxim odd)
An honest man's the noblest work of God;
If Pope's assertion be from error clear,
The noblest work of God is buried here.

Here lies an old soldier whom all should applaud,
He fought many battles at home and abroad;
But the hottest engagement he ever was in,
Was the battle of self in the conquest of sin.

1850.
In memory of James
and another son
who died in infancy
and five other friends
Erected by James Stewart,
Spirit merchant, Dundee,
and his spouse
and 3 other children.

At St. John's Worcester:
Honest John
's dead and gone.

A CONTRACTED EPITAPH.
Lo al y' eu' I spēt y' sū tme had I
Al y' I gaf I g°d ētēt y' nᵒw have I
Y' I neyIu' gaf ne lēt y, now abie I
Y' I kepe til I wēt y' lost I.
Lo, all that ever I spent, that sometime had I;
All that I gave in good intent, that now have I;
What I neither gave nor lent, that now suffer I;
That I kept till I went, that lost I.

Also, from Doncaster in Yorkshire:

> ⸸ Howe! Howe! who is heare?
> I Robin of Doncastere
> And Margaret my Flare (wife)
>   That I spent, that I had,
>   That I gave, that I have,
>   That I left, that I lost.
>   A. D. 1579.

Ruth Sprague, Daughter of Gibson and Elizabeth Sprague. Died June 11, 1846, aged 9 years, 4 months, and 3 days.

She was stolen from the grave by Roderick R. Clow, dissected at Dr. P. M. Armstrong's office, in Hoosick, N. Y., from which place her mutilated remains were obtained and deposited here.

> Her body dissected by fiendish man,
>   Her bones anatomized,
> Her soul, we trust, has risen to God,
>   Where few physicians rise.

GARDEN CITY CATHEDRAL, N. Y.

On the sarcophagus of A. T. Stewart, of New York City, whose body was stolen from St. Mark's churchyard:

"He is Not Here."

Norfolk, Conn:
>LIEUT. NATHAN DAVIS.
>Died in 1781.
>Death is a debt that's justly due,
>That I have paid and so must you.

>ELIZABETH, wife of NATHAN DAVIS.
>Died in 1786.
>This debt I owe is justly due,
>And I am come to sleep with you.

From Michaelchurch:

John Prosser is my name, and England is my nation,
Bowchurch is my dwelling place, and Christ is my salvation;
Now I'm dead and in my grave, and all my bones are rotten;
As you pass by remember me, when I am quite forgotten.

From Saint James, Long Island:
>He served the Lord,
>Obeyed His Voice,
>Hoped in His Word
>And died from Choice.

In the English Cathedral of Quebec, upon the left wall, is a tablet sacred to the memory of a lady " who died in the full hope of a resurrection after a short attack of Asiatic cholera."

From Lawrence, Long Island:
Letty Ann Mott.
Tho' her memory be written on earth,
  And her relics lie under the sod,
Recorded on high is her worth.
  She rests in the breast of her God.

From Grace churchyard, Jamaica, Long Island:
1746.
Her thread was short,
Her glass soon run,
Her sorrows o'er,
Her joys begun.

If wife, amazed! depart this holy **grave**,
Nor these new ashes ask, what names they have!
The graver in concealing them was wise,
For, whoso knows, straight melts in tears, and
    dies.

In the Grand Duke's Museum, Florence:
(Translated from the Latin.)
Philætius the son-in-law and
Duseris the stepmother,
who while living (you'll scarce believe it)
were unanimous, now they are dead
rest lovingly together in this Urn.

The world's a City full of crooked streets,
And death's the market place where all men meets.
If life was merchandise that men could buy,
The rich would always live, the poor would die.

Lived to the age of sixty-seven
Spurned at this earth and flew to heaven.

Near the rain spout of an old church:
Beneath the droppings of this spout
There lies the body once so stout,
Of Francis Thomson.

In Ely Cathedral:
Ursula Tindall by Birth;
Coxee by Choice;
Upcher for Age and Comfort.

Old English:
  Stay, Bachelor, if you have Wit,
    A wonder to behold!
  A husband and wife in one dark Pit,
    Lie close and never scold!
  Tread softly though, for fear she wakes —
    Hark! she begins already!
  "You've hurt my Head — my Shoulder akes;
    These Sots can ne'er move steady,"
  Ah Friend, with happy Freedom blest!
    See how my Hopes miscarried!
  Not Death itself can give you Rest,
    Unless you die unmarried.

John Anderson, Provost of Dundee, left in his will a sum of money to be given to the writer of a suitable epitaph. His three covetous executors agreed to each write a line of the epitaph and then divide the money bequeathed for that purpose among themselves.

They agreed that the beginning should be:

Here lies John Anderson, Provost of Dundee.

Then the three contributed their lines as follows:

  Here lies Him, here lies he.
  Hallelujah, Hallelujee!
  A-B-C-D-E-F-G!

Memorial stone in cemetery at Felchville, Vt.:
On the 31st of Aug., 1754, Capt. James Johnson had a daughter born on this spot of ground being captivated with his whole family by the Indians.

Indiana:

 ×He died at nashville tennessee
 he died of kronic diaree
 it trooly paneful must of bin
 to die so fur away from kin.

Arkansas. On a daughter of Mrs. Cabbage:
 Sweet bud of innocence, so soon decayed
 So soon lopped off in tenderest vegetation.

Milan, Ohio:

 ⨯ Dear Willie how we miss you,
 We miss your pleasant smile,
 Your kind little hand.
 We never shall see you,
 We never shall kiss you,
 Till we go to the promised land—
    Composed by his mother.

On a Crusader:

I, Fitzgivens Knight, having fought doughtily in the Holy Land, and hewed many circumsized infidels, now rest in peace. Odi Profanum.

On the Spartan defenders of Thermopylæ:

"Go, passenger, and tell at Lacedæmon, that we died in obedience to her sacred laws."

An ancient one much used:

Physicians were all in vain.

Requested by King Darius:

Here lies King Darius, who was able to drink many bottles of wine without staggering.

Milford, Conn., 1792. On a young lady aged twenty-four years:

Molly, though pleasant in her day,
Was suddenly seized and sent away,
How soon she's ripe, how soon she's rotten,
Laid in the grave and soon forgotten.

At Ahwaga on the Susquehanna River:
>   CHARLES LEWIS.
>   He voted for Abraham Lincoln.

Newton, Mass.:
>   CAPT. THOS. PRENTICE,
>   Died 1709.
> He that's here interred needs no versifying,
> A virtuous life will keep the name from dying.
> He'll live tho' poets cease their scribbling rhyme,
> When that this stone shall moulder'd be by time.

Baton Rouge, La.:
>   Here lies the body of David Jones.
>   His last words were:
>   I die a Christian and a Democrat.

On a very old tombstone in Middletown, Conn.:
>   Beautiful flower of Middletown
>   How art thou cutted down! cutted down!

Butler County, Ohio:

Here lies the woman, the first save one,
That settled on the Maine above Fort Hamilton,
Her table was spread, and that of the best,
And Anthony Wayne was often her guest.

Westminster Abbey:

Thomas Par of the County of Salop, born in Anno 1483. He lived in the reign of ten Princes, viz., Edward IV, King Edward V, King Richard III, King Henry VII, King Henry VIII, King Edward VI, Queen Mary, Queen Elizabeth, King James and King Charles. Aged 152 years, and was buried here Nov. 15, 1635.

On body of "Prodigium Willingamense" buried at Wellingham near Cambridge, England:

Stop traveller, and wondering know that here lie the remains of Thomas, son of Thomas and Margaret Hall. Before he was a year old, he arrived at puberty, and was near four feet high before he was three years old, endowed with great strength, exact symmetry of parts, and a stupendous voice. He had not quite reached his sixth year when he died, as of an advanced age. Here he was born and here he gave way to fate, September 3d, 1747.

In the Collatine way—at Rome:
      (Translation.)

To the Gods manes of sextos Perpenna Firmus. I lived as I liked, but why I died, I can give no reason.

    × Death takes the good—
        Too good on earth to stay;
    And leaves the bad—
        Too bad to take away.

Boston, Copp's Hill:
  ₓA sister of Sarah Lucas lieth here,
  Whom I did love most dear;
  And now her soul has took its flight,
  And bid her spiteful foes good-night.

Friends, as you pass, suppress the falling tear,
You wish her out of heaven to wish her here.

  So unafflicted, so composed a mind,
  So firm, yet soft, so young, yet so refined,
  Wasting disease and pain severely tried—
  The saint sustained it—but the woman died.

On a very wicked man who was killed by a fall from his horse:

> Between the stirrup and the ground,
> I mercy asked, I mercy found.

Woodland Cemetery, Phila.:

Two stones side by side have engraved the words:

>   Father   Mother

Connecting the two is an arch bearing the words:

> Divided in life—United in Death.

A man was buried between his two wives. Their head-stones have engraved hands with the fore-fingers pointing downward toward the husband's grave, and under each hand the words:

> He was ours.

On the husband's head-stone were two hands pointing to the two wives and underneath the words:

> They were mine.

On a Boston clergyman by himself:

Beneath this stone lies the body of one
Shamefully treated in life
By his wife's son and Dr. Thom
And Daniel Slavey's wife.

Sterling, Miss.:

As she on her bed of sickness lay,
  Her friends stood weeping around,
She not a word to them could say,
  No medicine could they get down.

Near this place
lies
CHARLES CLAUDIUS PHILLIPS
whose absolute contempt of Riches
& inimitable performance on
the Violin
made him the admiration of all
who knew him.

I, Jocky Bell o' Brackenbrow, lyes under this stane,
Five of my awn sons laid it on my wame,
I lived aw my deyes, but sturt or strife,
Was man o' my meat, and master o'er my wife;
If you've done better in your time than I did in mine,
Take the stane off my wame and lay it on thine.

On the tomb of a musical composer:

Here lies Sir John Hawkins
Without his shoes or his stawkings.

Here lies Elizabeth Wise,
She died of thunder sent from heaven
Seventy hundred and seventy-seven.

On the French Satirist Piron, by himself, having been refused admission to the French Academy:

Here lies Piron, who was nothing,
Not even an Academician.

On this marble drop a tear,
    Here lies fair Rosalind;
All mankind was pleased with her,
    And she with all mankind.

On Lady Dorothy Bellingham:

To labor born I bore, and by that form
I bore to earth, to earth I straight was borne.

Here rests a fine woman which was sent from above
To teach virtues and graces to men.
But God when he saw her in such very bad hands
Recalled her to Heaven again.

Over the grave of a wealthy Frenchman by his direction after having committed suicide:

    Tired of this eternal buttoning
        and unbuttoning.

At Ripple near Upton-on-Severn:

On a very tall man, seven feet four inches high, who died from over exertion in a contest to mow more hay than two other men:

As you pass by behold my length,
And never glory in your strength.

On a Trout, at Worcestershire, England:

IN
MEMORY
OF THE
OLD FISH.
UNDER THE SOIL
THE OLD FISH DO LIE
20 YEARS HE LIVED
AND THEN DID DIE.
HE WAS SO TAME
YOU UNDERSTAND
HE WOULD COME AND
EAT OUT OF OUR HAND.
DIED APRIL 20, 1855.
AGED 20 YEARS.

Epitaphs by "Max Adeler"

From "Out of the Hurly-Burly," by permission of the autho

Four doctors tackled Johnny Smith,
They blistered and they bled him
With squills and anti-bilious pills
And ipecac they fed him.
They stirred him up with calomel,
And tried to move his liver,
But all in vain,—his little soul,
Was wafted o'er the river.

The death angel struck Alexander McGl
And gave him protracted repose;
He wore a checked shirt and a No. 9 sho
And had a pink wart on his nose.

No doubt he is happier dwelling in space
Over there on the evergreen shore.
His friends are informed that his funeral
    takes place
Precisely at quarter past four.

Willie had a purple monkey
  Climbing on a yellow stick,
And when he sucked the paint all off
  It made him deathly sick;
And in his latest hours he clasped
  That monkey in his hand,
And bade good-bye to earth
  And went into a better land.

Oh no more he'll shoot his sister
  With his little wooden gun,
And no more he'll twist the pussy's tail
  And make her yowl, for fun.
The pussy's tail now stands out straight;
  The gun is laid aside;
The monkey doesn't jump around
  Since little Willie died.

EPITAPHS

We have lost our little Hanner, in a very painful manner,
And we often asked, How can her harsh sufferings be borne?
When her death was first reported, her aunt got up and snorted,
With the grief that she supported, for it made her feel forlorn.

She was such a little seraph that her father, who is sheriff,
Really doesn't seem to care if he ne'er smiles in life again,
She has gone, we hope, to heaven, at the early age of seven.
(Funeral starts off at eleven) where she'll nevermore have pain.

Oh! bury Bartholomew out in the woods
  In a beautiful hole in the ground,
When the bumble-bees buzz and the woodpeckers sing
  And the straddle-bugs tumble around.

So that, in winter, when the snow and the slush
   Have covered his last little bed,
His brother Artemus can go out with Jane
   And visit the place with his sled.

Mrs. McFadden has gone from this life;
   She has left all its sorrows and cares;
She caught the rheumatics in both of her legs,
   While scrubbing the cellar and stairs.
They put mustard plasters upon her in vain;
   They bathed her with whiskey and rum;
But Thursday her spirit departed, and left
   Her body entirely numb.

Little Alexander's dead;
   Jam him in a coffin;
Don't have as good a chance
   For a funeral often.
Rush his body right around
   To the cemetery;
Drop him in the sepulchre
   With his Uncle Jerry.

A man named Sparks who survived his four wives, had their bodies moved to a new cemetery lot. On the way the remains became hopelessly mixed, so that he found it necessary to inter all four in one grave, with this inscription:

> Stranger, pause, and shed a tear
> For Susan Sparks lies buried here
> Mingled, in some perplexing manner,
> With Jane, Maria, and portions of Hannah!

BIBLIOLIFE

Old Books Deserve a New Life
www.bibliolife.com

Did you know that you can get most of our titles in our trademark **EasyScript**™ print format? **EasyScript**™ provides readers with a larger than average typeface, for a reading experience that's easier on the eyes.

Did you know that we have an ever-growing collection of books in many languages?

Order online:
www.bibliolife.com/store

Or to exclusively browse our **EasyScript**™ collection:
www.bibliogrande.com

At BiblioLife, we aim to make knowledge more accessible by making thousands of titles available to you – quickly and affordably.

Contact us:
BiblioLife
PO Box 21206
Charleston, SC 29413

LaVergne, TN USA
17 November 2009
164311LV00007BC/2/A